Alistair Horne's work has been translated into ten languages, and he is the author of many bestselling books. They include *The Price of Glory: Verdun 1916*; *The Fall of Paris: The Siege and Commune 1870–81*; *Napoleon: Master of Europe 1805–1807*; *A Savage War of Peace: Algeria 1954–1962*; *How Far From Austerlitz? Napoleon 1805–1815*, *Seven Ages of Paris* and, in 2004, *The Age of Napoleon* and *Friend or Foe*. He was knighted in 2003 for services to Franco-British relations.

By Alistair Horne

Back into Power
The Land is Bright
Canada and the Canadians
The Price of Glory: Verdun 1916
The Fall of Paris: The Siege and the Commune 1870–71
To Lose a Battle: France 1940
The Terrible Year: The Paris Commune, 1871
Death of a Generation
Small Earthquake in Chile
Napoleon: Master of Europe 1805–1807
The French Army and Politics 1870–1970
A Savage War of Peace: Algeria 1954–1962
Macmillan: 1894–1956
Macmillan: 1957–1986
A Bundle from Britain
How Far from Austerlitz? Napoleon, 1805–1815
Seven Ages of Paris
The Age of Napoleon
Friend or Foe: An Anglo-Saxon History of France

The Lonely Leader: Monty 1944–45
(*with David Montgomery*)

Telling Lies
(*as editor*)

THE
TERRIBLE
YEAR

The Paris Commune, 1871

ALISTAIR HORNE

PHOENIX

A PHOENIX PAPERBACK

First published in Great Britain in 1971
by Macmillan London Ltd
This paperback edition published in 2004
by Phoenix,
an imprint of Orion Books Ltd,
Orion House, 5 Upper St Martin's Lane,
London WC2H 9EA

A CIP catalogue record for this book
is available from the British Library.

ISBN 1 84212 759 4

Typeset at The Spartan Press Ltd,
Lymington, Hants

Printed and bound in Great Britain by
Clays Ltd, St Ives plc

www.orionbooks.co.uk

For Vanessa – *encore!*

CONTENTS

Foreword to the 2004 Edition

There are two place names, bloody and grim by repute, which – perhaps above all others – have dominated French history over the past century and a half. One is Verdun, the appalling battle in 1916, which epitomised all that France suffered, and both won and lost in World War I. Nominally a glorious victory, the unacceptable cost – 400,000 men dead or mutilated on this one small corner of French soil – Verdun also led in a straight line to the demoralisation, and, ultimately, the crushing defeat of 1940. 'They will not be able to make us do it again another day,' wrote a young officer killed on that hideous battlefield. 'That would be to misconstrue the price of our effort. They will have to resort to those who have not lived these days.' In 1940 this prediction came true.

The other place is Père Lachaise Cemetery, at the east end of Paris. It was here, among its peaceful tombs and walks, that the Paris Commune expired in May 1871, in a welter of slaughter and executions. For many years afterwards, the Mur des Fédérés, where the last Communards were shot, remained a touchstone for the forces of the Left in France. No demonstration in Paris would be complete without it culminating at the Mur; and every May the Left and its adherents would march solemnly, sometimes hundreds of thousands strong, to commemorate the slain 'martyrs' of the Commune there.

To the Left, these 'martyrs' were seen as the natural heirs to the Revolutionaries of 1789, vanquished by the forces of reaction, and the French bourgeoisie.

In 1870, the brilliant late-afternoon sunshine of Louis-

Napoleon's Second Empire blinded most eyes to the disturbing realities of life beneath the surface. It was then totally inconceivable that, within the course of this one *Année Terrible*, as Victor Hugo characterised it, so proud and powerful a nation should have been catastrophically defeated in war, the centre of *la ville lumière* itself burnt down, and twenty thousand of its inhabitants slaughtered by their fellow countrymen.

The Commune ruled for a brief seventy days before expiring in a holocaust of fire and bloodshed far in excess of anything perpetrated during the Great Revolution of 1789, but it left behind an indelible mark that was to spread far beyond the boundaries of France.

With the hindsight of history, the Paris Commune appears as a classical model of revolution, totally predictable in its incidence. In common with the Russian Revolution of 1917 (for which Lenin made it serve as a dummy run), the Commune shared the same two basic causal antecedents – a long backlog of semi-submerged social and political discontent, and the sudden imbalance brought about by military defeat acting as a detonator to ignite it into a violent explosion.

When I first wrote *The Fall of Paris* in the 1960s, the story of the Siege and the Commune stood up as a subject of historical fascination in its own right, and it also formed the essential background to the trilogy I was trying to write on Franco-German rivalry. Even then the Commune part of the story, as a kind of last echo of 1793 and the first note of 1917, emerged as by far the more historically significant of the two events. This was before the students of Paris, chanting '*Vive la Commune!*', came close to re-enacting 1871 during the *événements* of 1968. Since then the Commune, beyond being – as always – an inspirational touchstone for Marxist revolutionaries the world over, has acquired a new relevance to the contemporary world.

Then, certain aspects of its short life – such as the taking and killing of hostages and urban warfare between guerrillas and regular forces – suddenly once again became sinister, and apparently insoluble facts of modern life in the 1970s. In Latin America, Left-wing 'Tupamaros' kidnapped foreign envoys, while in the Middle East Palestinians protesting the occupation of their lands by Israel introduced a new feature by hijacking international airliners. 'Who can predict', I wrote at the time

> that, in the 1970s, as the killing of hostages goes out of fashion, that other ingredient of the Commune – mass arson – may not take its place? Indeed, how much easier than hijacking an airplane it would be to burn down St Paul's – or Notre Dame and the Louvre that only escaped so narrowly a hundred years ago!

Who, indeed! Who, then, would have dared foresee what horrendous developments in the black art of Terror would lie ahead in the new century?

How far the wheel of fate has swung since, with the arrival on 9/11 of international terrorism on an unprecedented scale! The Communards, the fearless *pétroleuses* with their little bottles of arson may have helped point the way . . .

One of the incidental attractions of writing about *l'Année Terrible* originally was the marvellous articulateness of the eye-witnesses who were there: Hugo, Goncourt, Flaubert, Gautier, Daudet all wrote about it. The *richesse* of contemporary illustrations is equally imposing; apart from the talented war artists of the *Illustrated London News*, Daumier, 'Cham', Manet, Détaille and de Neuville were among the French artists who recorded the events of 1870–71.

In *The Fall of Paris*, I made wide use of published and unpublished accounts written by American and British neutrals present in Paris. They still seem to me to be among the best available, and I remain grateful to those correspondents (full acknowledgments are to be found in *The Fall of Paris*) who helped me in the first instance. I am also indebted to Messrs Macmillan for permitting me to requote passages from *The Fall of Paris*.

Alistair Horne
Turville, 2004

LIST OF ILLUSTRATIONS

— I —

SEDAN, 1870

'Having been unable to die in the midst of my troops, there is nothing left for me but to deliver my sword into Your Majesty's hands. I am Your Majesty's true brother. Napoleon.'

Simple, sad words, but they sealed an event of immeasurable consequences. It was 1 September 1870. A disastrous six-week campaign of unrelieved defeats inflicted by Moltke's Prussians, had brought Louis-Napoleon, nephew of the great Bonaparte, to bay in the small frontier fortress of Sedan. Here, after two days of bitter fighting, he had been forced to capitulate at the head of an army of a hundred thousand men.

The next day, acclaimed by one ragged last cheer of '*Vive l'Empereur!*' from loyal Zouaves, the last Emperor of the French – sick, and his face (it has been said) rouged to conceal the pain caused by an agonising stone on the bladder – disappeared into internment in a German fortress. The Prussian Army encamped around Sedan responded by bellowing forth Lutheran hymns of thanksgiving, then began to pack its equipment with jubilant shouts of '*Nach Paris!*'

'Untune one string, and hark what discord follows . . .' The breaking of the Imperial string, once seemingly so infrangible, could not help but induce deep discord in France, provoke an enduring cacophony in the centre of Europe. The capitulation at Sedan meant the shattering of the European order, intact since the settlement of 1815, and certainly the equilibrium of the continent was still not to be restored a century later. In France, revolutionary forces would shortly be released, which – though not successful in themselves – would serve as a paradigm and clarion call to later, more successful, Marxist-Leninist revolutionaries elsewhere.

On the outbreak of war that July, enthusiastic and excited crowds had swarmed through Paris, chanting '*À Berlin!*' and anticipating a speedy victory. If France was stunned by the suddenness and completeness of the ensuing defeats, the rest of the world had been equally taken by surprise. In London, when France had plunged into war (apparently on a mere triviality of etiquette), the betting had been strongly in her favour; though sympathies lay demonstrably with the about-to-be underdog. 'I would lay my last shilling on Casquette against Pumpernickel,' declared Delane of *The Times* – wrong as editors of that paper tend to be when it comes to assessing Germany – but fortunately for Delane nobody was prepared to accept his wager.

In fact, the military odds had been heavily on the other side. The Prussian Army of 1870 was a magnificent instrument by any standard. Although the population of Prussia and her German Allies totalled less than that of France, a reserve army system far in advance of the age enabled Moltke to muster an army of over a million men within eighteen days of mobilisation. Nothing like this had ever been seen in Europe before. Moltke, possibly a greater organiser than a strategist, had devoted his entire genius to the creation of the General Staff. For his huge body of troops it provided a brain and nerves such as no other nation possessed. No single item was left to chance. Railways built in Germany in recent years had all been planned with a particular eye to military needs, and a highly trained corps of telegraphists ensured excellent communications. All aimed at a maximum speed of concentration, for an offensive campaign that would hit the enemy hard before he was ready.

In weapons one or two French experts had noted with disquiet the monster 50-ton steel siege gun which had won a prize for Herr Krupp of Essen at the glittering Great Exhibition of Paris in 1867. Firing a shell approximately as heavy as two small French cannon, it was the biggest thing the world had ever seen. And military opinion had been startled, too, when

Moltke had trounced Austria in a staggeringly brief campaign the previous year.

Nevertheless, the French Army on the whole had not been disposed to take seriously the military pretentions of that nation of comic professors and beer-swilling bombasts. Yet by 1870 French military lore had advanced but little since the days of Jomini. The gay uniforms, the joyous fanfares, the scintillating breastplates of the Cuirassiers that had so often bedazzled Louis-Napoleon's ladies during the resplendent cavalcades at Longchamps belonged more to the First Empire than the world of the sober-looking Uhlans. France's generals – Bazaine, MacMahon, Canrobert, Bourbaki – had shown skill in chasing Algerians in Algeria, Mexicans (though less so) in Mexico, but by any criterion they were second-raters, with no experience of modern war against a European foe.

The new *chassepot* rifle possessed nearly twice the range of the Prussians' Dreyse 'needle-gun', but the French with their brass, muzzle-fed cannon had nothing to compare with the deadly steel breech-loading field artillery of Herr Krupp. Much faith was placed in a new secret weapon called the *mitrailleuse*, a kind of primitive machine-gun developed from the American Gatling; however, it was as large and vulnerable as a cannon, but without the latter's range; and it had been such a secret weapon that it was not to be issued until a few days before mobilisation.

When war came, France's mobilisation machinery, based on a faulty system of national service, had creaked into action amid scenes of dismal chaos. 'Have arrived at Belfort,' telegraphed one desperate general. 'Can't find my brigade. Can't find the divisional commander. What shall I do? Don't know where my regiments are.' Magazines were discovered to be empty. Gunners became separated from their guns. With superb Gallic self-confidence, the maps issued were of Germany, not France. Louis-Napoleon's plan, in so far as he had one, was to strike rapidly eastwards, in the hope of swinging the South German states into the war against their hectoring neighbour, Prussia. Across the Rhine, Moltke, ready with 400,000 troops in supreme fighting trim against the 250,000 partially organised men the Emperor had been able to muster, waited to see which way the enemy was going to jump. After a few preliminary skirmishes, he swiftly appreciated that the French Army had allowed itself to become divided by the line of the Vosges mountains. Concentrating his forces, first against one wing, then against the other, Moltke dealt each two hammer blows, at Wörth and Spicheren near the frontier.

Falling back in defeat, Bazaine found his retreat cut by fast-moving Prussian forces. After a day of most ferocious fighting at Gravelotte-St Privat, his army was forced to turn about and seek sanctuary under the guns of Metz; there to await reduction by siege. In a vain attempt to come to Bazaine's assistance at Metz, MacMahon set forth on the tragic march ending at Sedan, accompanied by the ailing Emperor himself. There, on the scene that was to produce another catastrophic failure of French arms just seventy years later, Louis-Napoleon was trapped and overwhelmed by two powerful Prussian armies.

Military inadequacy provides the immediate cause of this shattering defeat, but the deeper truth is to be sought in the various cankers that had been gnawing away for years at the social structure of the Empire. During its last years, Paris had never seemed more stunningly brilliant or prosperous; *la ville lumière*, really *the* centre of the civilised world, as arrogant in its dismissal of the 'rustics' misguidedly inhabiting the rest of France as it was in its contempt for the outside world. Dazzling balls, parades, and spectacles – the most successful of them being the Great Exhibition of 1867, when Paris had seemed to play host to the entire world – had followed each other in such quick succession that one critic accused the régime of being a 'government by spectacle'. They had blinded French eyes to the realities beneath the surface. Syphilis was rampant, and many of the great Frenchmen of the age were to die of it; Maupassant, Jules Goncourt, Dumas *fils*, Baudelaire, Manet. The dread disease was symptomatic of the Second Empire itself; on the surface, all gaiety and light; below, sombre purulence, decay and ultimately death.

Louis-Napoleon had been genuinely, and constructively,

dedicated to social reform and to creating internal prosperity (one traditional way of reconciling French minds to the removal of political liberties by an authoritarian régime). Under the Empire industrial production had doubled. Gold poured in from new mines in California and South Africa. Mighty banking concerns like the Crédit Lyonnais and the Crédit Foncier were established, the latter especially designed to stimulate the vast new building programme. The railway network increased from 3,685 to 17,924 kilometres; telegraph lines radiated out all over the country, and ship-building expanded as never before. Men like Monsieur Potin the grocer became millionaires overnight.

But somehow, for all Louis-Napoleon's good intentions, the workers – and, more particularly, the Parisian proletariat – had found themselves left out of the general wave of *enrichissez-vous*. Typically, company dividends at the Anzin collieries had tripled between 1852 and 1870, while the miner's pay-packet had increased by a mere 30 per cent. One unfortunate by-product of Prefect Haussmann's imaginative rebuilding of Paris was that rents for the workers had doubled, so that by 1870 they ate up one-third of their pay-packet; food could take another 60 per cent, which left very little over for the other good things of life. Indebtedness was general, so were drunkenness and child mortality.

According to Haussmann himself, in 1862 over half the population of Paris lived 'in poverty bordering on destitution' and a house described by the Goncourts in the Boulevard Magenta, where a poor woman was giving birth, was by no means unrepresentative of how that half lived: 'a room where the planks that form the walls are coming apart and the floor is full of holes, through which rats are constantly appearing, rats which also come in whenever the door is opened, impudent poor men's rats which climb on to the table, carrying away whole hunks of bread, and worry the feet of the sleeping occupants. In this room, six children; the four biggest in a bed; and at their feet, which they are unable to stretch out, the two smallest in a crate. The man, a costermonger, who has known better days, dead-drunk during his wife's labour. The woman, as drunk as her husband . . . And . . . an organ-grinder's monkey, imitating and parodying the cries and angry oaths of the shrew in the throes of childbirth, piddling through a crack in the rook on to the snoring husband's back!'

In his replanning of Paris, Haussmann had been motivated partly by aesthetics and the need to demolish the old plague-breeding spots of the medieval city, but also by simple security considerations. The fine, straight avenues of new Paris were to 'cut through the habitual storm centres' – and equally to provide superb fields of fire in case of trouble. In fact, they also resulted in concentrating the underprivileged into much larger slum areas, hatcheries of discontent and revolt like Belleville and Menilmontant. Their denizens still seethed in repressed anger at memories of Louis-Napoleon's *coup d'état* of December 1851, in the brutal aftermath of which 160 had been slaughtered on the streets of Paris, most of them workers, and 26,000 later arrested and transported in hulks. More politically conscious than any other, the Parisian proletariat had never forgiven Louis-Napoleon for destroying the Republic *they* had created; nor would they forget the way the *petit bourgeois* had betrayed them at the barricades of '51 – as indeed previously they felt they had been swindled out of their place in the sun after the uprisings of 1789, 1830 and 1848.

Only three ingredients were required to spark off a new and even more menacing explosion: a diminution of the vigilant police state, weapons and organisation.

The last, organisation, had progressed rapidly during the waning years of the Empire. Unions had been permitted under close police supervision, but out of sight French representatives had attended the first meeting of the International in 1863, promoted by Karl Marx, whose new and more violent teachings were beginning to replace, in France, those of the venerated Socialist, Proudhon. In 1867, the year of the dazzling Great Exhibition, the International held its second congress; *Das Kapital* was published, and supporters of Marx staged their first notable demonstrations in Paris.

The opponents of Louis-Napoleon, however, were by no means limited to the working classes. At one extreme were the 'respectable' Legitimists of the *haute bourgeoisie*, who wanted a Bourbon back on the throne, but principally there were the great mass of middle-class, 'moderate' Republicans, as represented in the veteran Adolphe Thiers and Jules Favre. More radical was the flamboyant young advocate, Léon Gambetta, and still further way-out among the extreme Left Republicans was Henri de Rochefort, a lapsed aristocrat possessed of the most vitriolic pen of the age. Then came a hotch-potch of dedicated revolutionaries; Jacobins, Blanquists, Proudhonists, Anarchists and later Internationalists. These included old hands like Delescluze and Blanqui, who between them had spent a total of forty-seven years in divers political prisons. Scattered among the opposition in its various layers were numerous intellectuals who hated the régime for its interference in their work, if not for more altruistic reasons. There were unquenchable crusaders like Daumier and exiled Victor Hugo, as well as painters like Renoir, Pissarro and Manet − whose *Dejeuner sur l'Herbe* had been among the 'new art' to be rejected by the square, philistine, bourgeois Establishment at the Great Exhibition. Above all there was the bibulous Courbet, who had flung back the Legion d'Honneur offered him in 1870.

Louis-Napoleon had sought in vain to palliate dissatisfaction at home with that steadfast panacea, the quest for *la gloire* in foreign fields. Russia, Italy, Luxembourg, Mexico − all disasters, and all had ended in his forfeiting friendships that might have been helpful in 1870. Inevitably this meddlesome foreign policy was bound to bring him into collision with Bismarck, who required a showdown with France in order to unite all the fragmented principalities of Germany under the mantle of Prussia.

In a final, desperate attempt to emasculate his adversaries, Louis-Napoleon had proclaimed the 'Liberal Empire' during the last year of his reign: running down the police state, lifting censorship and repealing restrictions on political meetings. But it was like the genie released from the bottle. The extremist

— 2 —

PARIS REVOLTS

The news of the capitulation at Sedan reached Paris after two days of contradictory rumours. 'Who can describe the consternation written on every face,' wrote Edmond de Goncourt in his journal: 'the sound of aimless steps pacing the streets at random, the anxious conversations of shopkeepers and concierges on their doorsteps, the crowds collecting at street-corners and outside town halls, the siege of the newspaper kiosks, the triple line of readers gathering around every gas lamp? . . . Then there is the menacing roar of the crowd, in which stupefaction has begun to give place to anger. Next there are great crowds moving along the boulevards and shouting: "Down with the Empire!" . . . And finally there is the wild, tumultuous spectacle of a nation determined to perish or to save itself by an enormous effort, by one of those impossible feats of revolutionary times.'

On the next day, 4 September, a beautiful sunny Sunday, Parisian churchgoers met companies of the National Guard heading for the Assembly, 'in steady silent march with drums beating'. The Paris National Guard was a kind of militia which, under the Second Empire, had originally been formed from the 'reliable' bourgeoisie, but with the disasters of war the Government had been forced to expand it on more democratic lines, and it was already well permeated with Republican sympathisers. Arriving at the Assembly, the Guards had little difficulty in penetrating the building – with agitators and leaders of the Left hanging on to their coat-tails. In a matter of minutes, the mob had invaded the Chamber itself, where they found the Deputies

9

of the Empire presciently packing up their belongings. In vain, 'moderate' Republican spokesmen tried to harangue the crowd; repeatedly the President called for order, then abandoned his seat.

At this moment of pandemonium, Jules Favre managed to propose judiciously 'it is not here, but at the Hôtel de Ville that we must proclaim the Republic'. There were good precedents; it was there that the revolutionary Municipal Government of Paris had been created in 1789, and there that the Provisional Government held sway in 1848.

Accordingly the excited crowds drew off to the Hôtel de Ville, headed by Favre, where they found an even more tense situation. The 'ultras' – or 'Reds' as they were to become better known – had already taken over, and were busy forming their own government, by means of dropping from the windows lists of names to the waiting mob, which then registered its approval of the names on the list. There threatened to be a first collision between the two sets of Republicans, until Favre – with a lawyer's ingenuity – placated the 'Reds' by proposing that the Government of the new Republic of France should be composed solely of Deputies from Paris. It now fell to Gambetta's fiery oratory to seize the imagination of the crowd by formally proclaiming the Republic.

The post of President fell to General Trochu, the Governor of Paris. A devoutly Catholic Breton, Trochu was a politically-minded soldier rather excessively given to long-winded speechifying, not noticeably a man of action, but he had been the only one of Louis-Napoleon's generals to emerge from the débâcle of the past six weeks with his reputation untarnished. He had certainly made no effort to preserve the previous régime, carefully locking himself up in his quarters until the storm was past. A pessimist by nature, Trochu accepted his new role reluctantly, having first been assured by his colleagues that they would 'resolutely defend religion, property and the family'. At a time when the nation was involved in a life-or-death struggle, it was perhaps a strange primary consideration.

The other key posts in the new Government were filled by

Favre, Gambetta, Ferry, Simon, Crémieux, Picard and Arago. All had spent a lifetime in hopeless and helpless opposition; they had been swept into power before being able to formulate any united policy or forward strategy; and by conviction they were kindly-minded liberals, not revolutionary Dantons. Fundamentally theirs was a weak position in that they had no other title to be in power than the acclaim of the Paris mob. Conspicuously absent from this line-up was any member of the 'Red' faction; only the rabble-rousing Rochefort received a sinecure job, by way of muzzling him. It was an omission that would soon prove a source of grave trouble, with the 'Reds' constantly taunting the Government that it regarded its chief function as being to maintain the bourgeois *status quo*, as much as to make war on the Prussians. The charge would contain more than a grain of truth.

At the same time, as in the case of past revolutions, France was now ruled by a Government formed by Parisians, and for Parisians. The views of the rest of the country had never been considered for one moment.

That night the Empress Eugénie was smuggled out of a side door of the Louvre by two ambassadors, eventually to reach England, where she spent the remainder of a long, sad life. Soon after her departure, the Paris mob invaded the Tuileries Palace, ripping down imperial eagles, and joyfully hurling busts of the deposed Emperor into the Seine. Thus ended the Second Empire.

The first step the new Government took – with great courage, but against every logic – was to announce its determination to continue the war to the bitter end. 'This is the third awakening; and it is beautiful beyond fancy,' rejoiced sixty-six-year-old George Sand. 'Hail to thee, Republic! Thou art in worthy hands, and a great people will march under thy banner after a bloody expiation.' Somehow, as an article of faith, ignoring the approach of the terrible Prussians, everyone on the boulevards seemed to *believe* that all was going to turn out all right – now that France was a Republic again.

In particular, a new patriotism infused the Paris proletariat.

Instead of there being simply an 'unjust' war between two princes, the sacred Republic was now threatened by an invading foreign tyrant – just as it had been at Valmy. In the glowing autumn sunshine, a strange state of euphoria seized all Paris. 'The army fraternised with the citizens,' observed a young Englishman, Edwin Child 'carrying the butt end of their muskets in the air, and the town presented more the appearance of a grand national *fête*, than that of the capital of a country that has just received the shock of the greatest capitulation and defeat known in history.'

For anyone in the know, the prospects, however, were hardly promising. With a quarter of a million men captive or besieged, little enough remained of the army Louis-Napoleon had taken to the wars six weeks previously. It was clear that the forces available would be inadequate to prevent the Prussians from investing Paris. But, protected by strong city ramparts and an outer network of well-sited and powerful forts some forty miles in circumference the fortified city would be a tough nut to crack with the weapons of 1870. Accordingly Trochu prepared for siege.

The forces for the defence of Paris were slim enough: some 3,000 cannon of all sizes; perhaps 60,000 regulars of mixed quality, including two good regiments; a smattering of naval gunners; plus some hundred thousand *Mobiles*, partly trained Territorials from the provinces, many of whom had no high regard for the city-dwellers of Paris. Then there was the Paris National Guard. Numbering only 24,000 volunteers at the outbreak of war, it had been expanded first to 90,000, and now Trochu vastly augmented it by introducing compulsory registration. The Guard was paid 1.50 francs a day and – as a sop to the 'Reds' of Belleville – was allowed to elect its own officers. To everyone's astonishment, the enrolment of the Guard quickly produced some 350,000 able-bodied males, a fact which in itself revealed the inefficiency of France's wartime mobilisation. Arm these ardent Parisians, thought Trochu, and here could be an invaluable body for the city's defence; but no more than King Husain of Jordan did he reckon on what an element of future calamity these armed 'irregulars' would become.

A small army of labourers was set to work improving the fortifications. Goncourt, visiting the ramparts in September, noted activity everywhere: 'Throughout the length of the road, the manufacture of fascines, gabions, sand-bags, and in the trenches the digging of powder magazines and petroleum stores. On the paving of the former customs barracks, the dully echoing thud of cannon-balls tumbling off waggons. Above, on the ramparts, gunnery practice by civilians; below, musketry by the National Guard. The passage of silent groups of workers; the passage of the blue, black and white blouses of the *Mobiles*; and in a kind of grassy canal where the railway runs, the flashing past of trains with only their superstructures visible, red with military trousers, stripes, epaulets and caps of this completely martial population, improvised in the midst of the bourgeois population.'

In the beautiful Bois de Boulogne trees were felled to make barricades and provide fuel; while into the Bois and every park in Paris, herdsmen brought cattle and sheep gathered up from many miles around the city. 'As far as ever the eye can reach,' wrote a British correspondent in Paris, 'over every open space, down the long, long avenue all the way to Longchamp itself, nothing but sheep, sheep, sheep! The South Downs themselves could not exhibit such a sea of wool.'

Vaguely the Trochu Government reckoned it would have enough food to last the two million Parisians for eighty days. But well before this time surely some unspecified miracle would have brought new armies, or allies, to relieve the *ville lumière?*

Within weeks, a truly remarkable transformation had occurred in Paris. No longer was there a smell of defeat in the air. 'If you saw Paris today, you would be astonished,' wrote Louis Péguret to his mother in the provinces. 'It's no longer a city, it's a fortress, and its squares are nothing more than parade-grounds. Everything is cluttered up with soldiers and *Mobiles* carrying out manoeuvres in rivalry against each other.'

This new-found martial bravado had its unpleasant aspects;

one of them, a mounting obsession for discovering Prussian 'spies'. One Englishman saw National Guardsmen drag off some poor woman, crying 'It's Madame de Bismarck!' From this he concluded: 'it was positively dangerous for any flat-breasted female of more than ordinary height, and with the suspicion of down on her upper lip, to venture on the streets!'

A wild-eyed optimism briefly gripped the volatile city. America – the first nation to do so – recognised the new Republic, and the Bourse fluttered cheerfully upwards as Italy, Spain, and Switzerland followed suit. Returning from exile, that vigorous septuagenarian, Victor Hugo, typified the mood in addressing an eloquently arrogant appeal to the Prussians: 'It is in Paris that the beating of Europe's heart is felt. Paris is the city of cities. Paris is the city of men. There has been an Athens, there has been a Rome, and there is a Paris . . . Is the nine-teenth century to witness this frightful phenomenon? A nation fallen from polity to barbarism, abolishing the city of nations; Germans extinguishing Paris. . . . Can you give this spectacle to the world? Can you, Germans, become Vandals again?'

— 3 —

THE FIRST SIEGE BEGINS

But the Germans were not disposed to be impressed. Moltke's forces were now closing in on the capital irresistibly fast, sustained by a consumption of looted wine so enormous that America's General Sheridan accompanying them reported 'two almost continuous lines of broken bottles along the roadsides all the way down from Sedan'. On 17 September, the vanguard of some hundred-and-fifty thousand Prussian infantry and cavalry reached Paris, then – like the claws of a crab – started their enveloping movement. Two days later the Paris garrison launched the Republic's first major action since Sedan against the enemy approaching the key Chatillon heights south of Paris. It was led by the peppery General Ducrot, who had escaped from his captors at Sedan – always ready to do battle, and himself infected with the new spirit of optimism in Paris.

Alas, Ducrot's attack was greeted with no more success than any battle fought by Louis-Napoleon. Under heavy fire, a battalion of the renowned Zouaves (many of them in fact young recruits) broke and ran. Fugitives from the battle soon reached the streets of Montparnasse, where Goncourt encountered some of them: 'They said that they were all that remained of a body of two thousand men. . . . Farther away, a terrified *Mobile* was relating that the Prussians numbered a hundred thousand in the Bois de Meudon. . . . One senses in all these accounts the madness of fear, the hallucinations of panic . . .'

Furious, Ducrot was forced to fall back inside the Paris fortifications. The next day, 20 September, the two Prussian claws met near Versailles, which surrendered without a shot.

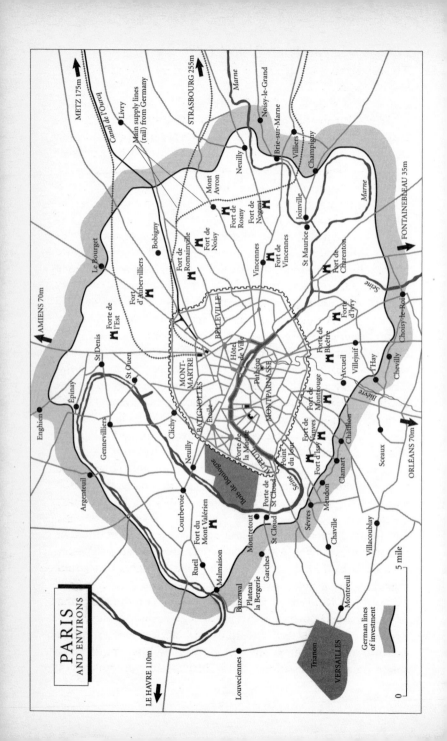

PARIS
AND ENVIRONS

METZ 175m

STRASBOURG 255m

Main supply lines
(rail) from Germany

Canal de l'Ourcq

Livry

Marne

Noisy-le-Grand

Brie-sur-Marne

Villiers

Champigny

Neuilly

Mont
Avron

FONTAINEBLEAU 35m

Marne

Joinville

Fort de
Rosny

Fort de
Nogent

Bobigny

Fort de
Noisy

St Maurice

Fort de
Charenton

Fort de
Romainville

Vincennes

Fort de
Vincennes

Le Bourget

Fort
d'Aubervilliers

Seine

AMIENS 70m

Forte de
l'Est

BELLEVILLE

Forte
d'Ivry

Choisy-le-Roi

St Denis

Hôtel
de Ville

Porte de
Bicêtre

MONT-
MARTRE

Panthéon

Villejuif

l'Hay

Chevilly

Épinay

Clichy

BATIGNOLLES

MONTPARNASSE

Arcueil

Enghien

St Ouen

Étoile

Fort de
Montrouge

ORLÉANS 70m

Bièvre

Gennevilliers

Neuilly

Porte de
la Muette

Fort de
Vanves

Fort d'Issy

Point
du Jour

Chatillon

Argenteuil

Courbevoie

Bois de Boulogne

Porte de
St Cloud

Seine

Clamart

Sceaux

Fort du
Mont Valérien

Montretout

St Cloud

Sèvres

Meudon

Villacoublay

LE HAVRE 110m

Rueil

Malmaison

Garches

Chaville

Montreuil

Buzenval

Plateau
la Bergerie

Louveciennes

Trianon

VERSAILLES

German lines
of investment

0   5 mile

The siege was set. Paris was now completely severed from the rest of France.

The poor showing of the Zouaves at Chatillon strengthened in Trochu's naturally pessimistic mind doubts he had begun to hold about the efficacy of the troops under his command, for all the apparent rise in morale, when confronted by Moltke's Prussians. Henceforth he would view any major offensive out of Paris with the greatest reserve. The city might itself withstand assault, but it was clear that relief could only come from outside. Therefore a kind of Churchill was required to inspire and re-arm the provinces, and bring them to the assistance of the capital. And quickly! But was there a Churchill among France's new leaders, and even if there was, how could he be got out of besieged Paris?

A possible answer to the second question was sent, literally, from above. A number of balloons had been located in Paris, some of them left-overs from the Great Exhibition of 1867, and most of them in disrepair. One, however, the *Neptune*, had been sufficiently patched up to be wafted out of Paris on 23 September, carrying 125 kilogrammes of dispatches safely over the heads of the astonished Prussians. Four other balloons took off in quick succession, with equal success. The blockade seemed to have been broken, and a reliable means established for communicating with the provinces.

As soon as the idea was mooted of ballooning a plenipotentiary to Tours to organise the provinces, the dauntless Ducrot volunteered. But Trochu considered him indispensable in Paris. Few others in the Government had quite matched Ducrot's enthusiasm; Favre turned positively green, and Rochefort became unusually silent. 'Monsieur Gambetta,' wrote Trochu with commendable honesty, 'was the only one of us who could regard without apprehension the prospects of a voyage in a balloon.' As Minister of the Interior, Gambetta did seem the logical choice. His other talents were then perhaps less evident. The son of an Italian grocer, he was only thirty-two and of an extremely unpromising appearance. His morals were question-able – possibly the cause of his black beard and mane of unkempt hair having turned prematurely grey. But already he had established himself as one of the great orators of France, and above all his meridional blood endowed him with something notably lacking in the other men about Trochu – passion.

On 8 October, a favourable wind enabled Gambetta to start on his epic flight. A huge crowd had assembled round a launching-pad set up in the Place St Pierre, Montmartre, the highest point of Paris and close to where the Sacre-Cœur now stands. Wrapped up in a great fur cloak prepared by some kind feminine hand, Gambetta climbed into the open wicker basket. His normally florid face was pale, understandably so. To embark on this kind of balloon journey in 1870 probably required as much real courage as for a Borman or an Armstrong a hundred years later; for the balloonists there were no batteries of computers on earth, ready to guide them down, nor flotillas standing by to pick them out of the sea; while over their head billowed a great bag of highly inflammable coal-gas that needed just one stray enemy bullet to turn it into a ball of flame.

With a fine sense of theatre, Gambetta recovered his nerve sufficiently to unfurl a tricolour as the anchor ropes were cast off. The *Armand Barbès* began to rise, spinning and jigging with a sickening motion, accompanied by great cries of '*Vive la France! Vive la Republique!*' Flying dangerously low over the Prussian lines, Gambetta made one abortive attempt to land, and his hand was grazed by a Prussian bullet. But eventually he arrived safely at Tours, where, within forty-eight hours, he had established himself as a virtual dictator, issuing inflamed proclamations to call the provinces to arms. It was the beginning of France's 'finest hour' of the war.

Meanwhile, in Paris the reverse suffered by Ducrot administered a sharp corrective to the mood of almost hysterical optimism that had swept the city along since the revolt of 4 September. 'The streets and people are very quiet,' wrote Edwin Child. 'All that enthusiasm has cooled down. Were it not for the enormous consumption of newspapers the difference of Paris ordinary and in a state of siege would be almost imperceptible.'

As September gave way to October, it became apparent that the Prussians were not going to try to seize Paris by brutal assault. In the hearts of the mercurial Parisians, optimism gave way to relief, and relief in turn to boredom: *l'ennui*, that most dangerous of French diseases! The theatres and the opera had closed their doors; a ten o'clock curfew had been imposed, and the gay streets of the *ville lumière* had become so dark and deserted that they reminded people of London.

'To live within oneself,' wrote Goncourt on 15 October, 'to have no other exchange of ideas than something as undiverse and limited as one's own thought, rotating around one obsession; to read nothing but thoroughly predictable news about a miserable war; . . . to be deprived of all that provided recreation for the mind of educated Paris; . . . finally, to vegetate in this brutal and monotonous state of affairs, war, thus is the Parisian imprisoned in Paris by a boredom comparable to that of a provincial city.'

Bad enough for Goncourt, but among those not endowed with the self-reliance of the intellectual *l'ennui* could induce far more explosive psychoses.

— 4 —

'RED' MURMURINGS

By way of compensation for boredom and the lack of news from the outside world, the wildest rumours began to circulate in Paris:

— The Prussians are in retreat towards the coast.
— The Duc d'Aumale is advancing from Le Havre at the head of a new army.
— Sheep and cattle are pouring into the city through a secret tunnel.
— Moltke is dead! The Crown Prince is dying!
— England has declared war on Prussia.
— Revolution in Berlin!

As the weeks went by, and all these heartening rumours proved baseless, boredom naturally turned to disillusion with Trochu's Government. Why was it not doing something to break the Prussian grip on Paris? Discontent was growing particularly on the extreme Left, among the 'Reds', who had not been invited to participate in the new Government. Bad as they had been under Louis-Napoleon, conditions for the poor were now worse than ever.

But more than any other section of the populace, the Parisian proletariat was still dedicated – and would remain dedicated – to continuing the war *à outrance*. To the property-owning and commercial classes, the war as it dragged on was bound to signify a waste of material assets. These were things the proletariat had never possessed; for them it was Paris, the holy city of revolution, that was threatened, and if it fell to the King of

Prussia he would doubtless restore his fellow despot, the hated Emperor. As Dantonesque memories were revived of how the foreign interventionists had been repelled in 1792, so for the first time there began to be heard clamours for the rebirth of a Commune de Paris which, like its famous predecessor, would in some mystical way repeat the miracle.

The uneasy truce between the 'Reds' and 'moderates' had expired with the débâcle at Chatillon. Angry voices on the Left were now raised against the Government. While Rochefort was in the Government, his *Lanterne* was fairly restrained; but there was Blanqui's *La Patrie en Danger* and *Le Réveil* of Delescluze, and the most scurrilous of all was Félix Pyat's *Le Combat*. Pyat was a professional revolutionary, once described as 'the purest romantic terrorist that ever flung a paper-bomb', who – like his two colleagues – had spent much of his sixty years in prison. His experience had given him a remarkable sixth sense, which somehow enabled him to turn up invariably at the critical moment of a revolution or conspiracy; more remarkable still was his facility for disappearing when things went wrong. Reappearing in Paris after long exile in London, he had started *Le Combat* on 16 September, immediately launching into virulent attack on the Trochu Government, which was to set the tone for the rest of the Left-wing press.

Accused of every kind of soft-pedalling, ill-faith, and – worse – treachery, Trochu and the bourgeois elements he represented were charged with being poised to do a deal with the enemy: 'the Government of the so-called National Defence has had only one thought; peace,' declared Blanqui on 22 September. 'Not a victorious peace, not even an honourable peace, but peace at any price . . . it does not believe in resistance . . .'

And now a source of power potential such as the Paris extremists had never known before was there to lend immense amplification to their voices. The inflated National Guard had rapidly established itself as *the* storm centre of the Left. In the minds of its more rosy-spectacled progenitors, expansion of the *Garde* was designed to fulfil three functions: it would quickly produce a mass of trained soldiers; the 'thirty sous' daily pay would provide relief for the poor of Paris, now confronted with widespread unemployment; and it would keep the 'Reds' quiet by giving them an outlet for their bellicosity. But in only the second respect had these hopes shown any likelihood of vindication. Undoubtedly the 'thirty sous' saved many poorer Parisians from starvation during the siege, but, as a British correspondent predicted, they would 'constitute a formidable difficulty when the war is over, for the recipients have already come to consider they have a right to State pay, and will strongly resist its withdrawal'.

To command the National Guard, Trochu had appointed General Tamisier, an elderly regular with no great force of character. The leader of one of the Belleville battalions, the flamboyant Flourens, dismissed him scornfully as 'a fine old man, of the stamp of a retired grocer, who must twenty years ago have had some energy'. In the 'Red' battalions, the real power lay in the hands of the demagogues; for, the Government having foolishly granted them the right to elect their own officers, they almost invariably handed the top ranks to the soapbox orators and red-hot revolutionaries, regardless of any military qualifications.

Uniforms of the *Garde* presented an extraordinarily motley: some battalions were clad in chocolate brown, some in brilliant green, and in the earliest days they mounted watch on the ramparts in anything from tartan to sheepskins. Some of the smarter units from the bourgeois *arrondissements* provided themselves with seductive young *cantinières*, got up like the regimental daughters of comic opera. On one occasion a 'curious-looking' colonel arriving to inspect a unit was exposed as a woman – the mistress, in fact, of the real colonel, who had not wished to break up his game of cards. Discipline was certainly not impressive, and therefore it was perhaps hardly surprising that Trochu had been extremely wary about allowing it to perform anything but the simplest military tasks: 'They make holes and fill them with spikes; sow their ramparts with nails, points upwards, and propose even to cover these with broken glass, as if the Prussians were so many cats.'

To the *Gardes*, the sense of their uselessness was understandably demoralising, and for many drink provided the inevitable refuge. The poet, Paul Verlaine, just recently married, was one whose surrender to alcohol stemmed from these futile days on the ramparts. You could buy a lot of cheap wine on 1.50 francs a day, and besides it kept you warm. So the *Garde* spent its days in the bistros, and it was by no means unusual to see them marching to their posts in crooked, erratic lines.

Next to drink, the best way of keeping warm was by listening to wild, inflammatory polemics against the Government, the bourgeoisie and private property in general, in the super-heated, sulphurous atmosphere of the Red Clubs – 'the theatres and *salons* of the people'. The output of sheer nonsense from the Clubs was quite remarkable. There was always a strong element of anti-religious obsession, and frequent declarations in favour of free love. Fervid ideas were generated on how the Government could win the war, interspersed with even more inspired inventions, such as *escargots sympathiques* which were to carry messages in their shells through the Prussian lines. There was remarkably little time for serious discussion of such unmilitary topics as Socialism. But any orator could be assured of frenzied applause whenever he compared the timidity and indecision of the men of 4 September with the ruthlessness of '93; or whenever he mentioned the Terror, or the mystical Commune.

One of the 'darlings' of the Red Clubs was Gustave Flourens, the son of an illustrious physician, with a brilliant academic brain himself, and about the same age as Gambetta. A Byronic knight-errant in the service of Liberty, whatever its name and however Utopian, Flourens had gone to Crete to fight against the Turks. But evidently the Greeks had found him too troublesome, and he narrowly escaped being deported back to France. After he had drifted home again, involvement in an inept conspiracy against Louis-Napoleon had landed him in gaol. Hardly had he been released than he found himself in a duel with one of the best swordsmen of the day, and was nearly killed. After 4 September, his swaggering allure, eloquence and sheer panache promptly gained him leadership of the five

Belleville battalions of the *Garde*, although there was nothing proletarian about him. He wore magnificently embroidered Grecian-style uniforms of his own design (with badges of rank one higher than he was entitled to), and had commandeered two of the finest mounts of the Imperial stables. Fair-haired, with commanding blue eyes, a beard and flowing red mustachios, he was a notable consumer of women, and also – unlike many of his fellow revolutionaries – a man of action.

'The blood was boiling in our veins, the earth burning under our feet,' declared Flourens, and certainly *his* blood was beginning to boil over at the inaction of Trochu's Government. On 5 October, Flourens's patience reached breaking point, and at the head of the Belleville National Guard, accompanied by bands blaring, he marched to the Hôtel de Ville. Here he presented to Trochu various heterogeneous demands, in the name of the whole National Guard, and headed with a call for an immediate sortie by the *Garde*. Trochu treated the rebellious major with a mildness that shocked his aides, remonstrating gently, 'I could be your father. Your place is on the ramparts, and not at the Hôtel de Ville.'

Finally, Flourens withdrew quietly; but not before the *Garde* had thoroughly booed both Trochu and their own commander, General Tamisier. Three days later, a second, less disciplined march was made on the Hôtel de Ville, led by a wild-eyed figure called Sapia. This time Flourens prudently played no part, and this time Trochu had some 'loyal' Guards from the bourgeois *arrondissements* standing by. There was a moment of ugly confrontation, then Sapia was seized and bundled off, and rain dispersed the militants. But, on this occasion, the atmosphere was more one of revolt than of demonstration, and for the first time cries of '*Vive la Commune!*' were heard outside the Hôtel de Ville.

The following day Blanqui in his *La Patrie en Danger* was predicting, not without accuracy, that henceforth 'the good Germans will await phlegmatically the end of our cattle and our flour. After which, the Government of National Defence will declare in unison that Paris has defended herself heroically, and that it is now time to think of the *pot-au-feu* . . . 8 October will mark in history the day that the first article of the Capitulation of Paris was written by bourgeois bayonets.'

Summing up these two discouraging events, Labouchere – Britain's 'Besieged Resident' in Paris – commented gloomily: 'What will be the upshot of this radical divergence of opinion between the two principal classes which are cooped up together within the walls of Paris it is impossible to say.'

THE HÔTEL DE VILLE INVADED

Given the natural impatience of the Gallic character, it was hardly to be expected that Flourens should remain the only one to break the bonds of inactivity. On 27 October, an ambitious brigadier-general called de Bellemare, commanding a sector of the flat plain north of Paris, decided – on his own initiative – to have a crack at the village of Le Bourget, close to the site of today's airport. Sent in on a night attack, a detachment of 250 *francs-tireurs* caught a company of the Prussian Guard napping, and – rather to his astonishment – de Bellemare found himself in possession of Le Bourget. Having despatched two extra battalions of reinforcements, he then set off to Paris to report his success to Trochu, and (according to the latter) to request he accordingly be promoted *général de division*.

Trochu was displeased, telling de Bellemare that the village was both inessential and indefensible (which was correct), and that his indisciplined action was only 'increasing the death roll for nothing at all'. Meanwhile, the Paris press, thirsty for a triumph at any cost, had at once proclaimed it the first great victory of the siege. But while de Bellemare was absent, pressing his suit for promotion, the Prussians counter-attacked in force. The French fought back bravely, and the action degenerated into house-fighting, becoming one of the most savage of the war. By midday on the 30th Le Bourget was once again in Prussian hands after a gallant last-ditch resistance in the little church of St Nicholas. (Today the gloomy little church still stands on the way to the airport, with traces of Prussian bullets and its walls hung with primitive murals commemorating the battle.) De Bellemare's action (he did eventually get his promotion) cost the French nearly 1,200 men, the Germans only 477. In Paris, the dolour suffered by dashed hopes was extreme.

Yet, before the full impact of the defeat at Le Bourget could be felt, another sledge-hammer blow of even worse news came down on top of it. After a two months' siege, Bazaine surrendered at Metz on 29 October. The last of Louis-Napoleon's armies, 6,000 officers and 173,000 men, marched out, ragged, sick and hungry, and many wretchedly and sullenly drunk. As Bazaine himself rode forth into captivity, women spat at him, and immediately the news reached Tours, Gambetta had Bazaine proclaimed a traitor. A whole new Prussian army was now free to join in besieging Paris, or to deal with Gambetta.

As early as the 27th, Pyat had headlined Le Combat 'FALL OF METZ'. The Government promptly denounced the story, stigmatised the paper a 'Prussian organ', and outraged citizens had burned Le Combat on the streets. Then, on 31 October, the truth of Le Combat's report was officially admitted. On hearing the news, a patriotic Frenchwoman, Juliette Lambert, declared: 'I cannot express the chagrin, the discouragement, the rage and despair which invaded me, I slumped into a chair without knowing where I was.' In disgust, Rochefort – the Left's one voice in the Government – resigned his post.

Then, as a third and final shock to the guerre à outrance faction, it was revealed that Thiers had returned from abroad with an armistice proposal, and was in fact urging the Government to accept the latest Prussian terms, which included the cession of Alsace. The word quickly got around the Left-wing strongholds that a 'peace at any price' sell-out was being prepared by that old enemy of the working class. The Mayor of Montmartre, a fiery young radical called Georges Clemenceau, that morning posted up an affiche declaring: 'The municipality of the 18th Arrondissement protests with indignation against an armistice which the Government could not accept without committing treason.'

Coming in such swift succession, the combined force of the three blows shocked bourgeois Paris and was altogether too much for the Paris 'Reds'. On the afternoon of 'Black Monday' – which happened to be Hallowe'en – the storm broke.

Early that morning, Parisians were aroused by 'a rather stronger storm of drums and trumpets . . . than even we have been accustomed to during the last six weeks. . . . Thousands of National Guards were marching in every direction, and as they were not, as a rule, in heavy marching order, were too clean to be coming from, and too late to be going to, the forts or fortifications, it struck us that something was in the air. . . . I marched off at once to the Hôtel de Ville. As I passed along the Rue de Rivoli, I saw on every side the signs of a brewing storm. All the concierges were outside their gates, and their wives, who should have been "doing the first floor" were talking to other conciergeresses, who should have been "doing" the "entresol" and the "second". Men in trousers with red stripes were carefully putting up their shutters.'

The Hôtel de Ville was surrounded by an angry and excited mob. Amidst a tremendous din, individual shouts of 'No armistice!' and 'Down with Trochu!' were drowned out by raucous blasts of bugles, and occasional unison chants of '*Vive la Commune!*' Inside, the seat of Government had in fact already been seized by surprise by insurgent 'Red' National Guards. A Cabinet meeting, headed by Trochu, was in session in the elegant *Salon Jaune*, when suddenly outside there was a flurry of trumpets; the doors flew open, and in strode Flourens, superbly booted and spurred and carrying a great Turkish scimitar. Behind him came Blanqui, Delescluze, Pyat, Millière, and most of a new 'Government' drawn up that morning in Belleville.

To make himself heard above the hubbub, Flourens leaped up onto the conference table. Up and down it he strode, issuing orders right and left, calling for Trochu to resign, kicking over inkwells, and scuffing up the green baize with his spurs, his boots on a level with Trochu's nose. With remarkable sang-froid, the outraged President continued to sit there, imperturbably puffing at his cigar, with a Gioconda-like smile on his lips.

For the rest of the day, this extraordinary situation continued, with the Government a prisoner of the 'Reds'. As on 4 September, a snowstorm of paper slips was showered on the expectant mob below, bearing names of candidates for the new 'Government'. But soon the 'Reds' were split by argument and indecision – revealing their lack of planning behind the coup of that day, as well as their inherent disorganisation that was to feature so largely in bringing them to disaster the following spring. Swiftly the insurgents broke up into groups and caucuses to decide on a new leader. As Lissagaray, the 'official' historian of the Commune, wrote: 'thus that day which could have revitalised the defence vanished in a puff of smoke. The incoherence of the *avant-garde* restored to the Government its virginity of September.' Tempers rose; Blanqui declined to have Flourens on his 'list' and Delescluze would not have Pyat. Meanwhile, looted wine from the cellars was also having its effect on the rank and file.

Outside, to apprehensive bourgeois Parisians watching the scene like Goncourt, the spectacle of 'the workers who had led the movement of 4 September sitting on the sills with their legs dangling outside' told them the worst: 'The Government had been overthrown and the Commune established. . . . Today one could write: *Finis Franciae.* . . .' With superb irrelevance, Goncourt was asked by an old lady in the crowd if 'the price of Government stock was quoted in my paper'. Gloomily he speculated: 'Civil war, with starvation and bombardment, is that what tomorrow holds in store for us?' His pessimism was shared by the astute American Minister, Elihu Washburne, who concluded that evening that 'the revolution had been practically accomplished, and that we should have a genuine Red Republic'.

But in fact, amid the confusion reigning within the Hôtel de Ville and in the semi-darkness as night closed in, a loyal posse of National Guardsmen had managed to 'kidnap' Trochu, and smuggle him out of the building. Reaching his office in the Louvre, Trochu discovered that his fiery lieutenant, Ducrot, was already on his way into the centre of Paris, at the head of a powerful force and on his own initiative. Fearful of the blood-shed that might ensue, Trochu tried – unsuccessfully – to head him off. On arriving at the Louvre, Ducrot angrily told Trochu that the Government 'had to act immediately with energy, crush the insurgents and liberate their prisoners by force'. He begged him to let his men fire into the mob; he could disperse it in five minutes. Trochu refused; extreme methods were to be shunned, the Ministers still held by the insurgents – Favre, Simon, Dorian, Arago and others – should be liberated by negotiation, and repressive measure postponed until the morrow.

Finally, a compromise was produced. The 'loyal' National Guard would alone march to surround the Hôtel de Ville; while at the same time two battalions of *Mobiles*, notably Bretons, that were housed in the nearby Napoleon Barracks would carry out an ingenious Trojan-horse tactic. There was, as one of Trochu's staff pointed out, a subterranean tunnel some one hundred yards long linking the barracks with the Hôtel de Ville, built by Napoleon I so that the Hôtel de Ville could be garrisoned against an uprising within five minutes.

So the bizarre day ended on a note of the Arabian Nights. Down the secret subterranean passage the *Mobiles* crept, lighting their way with resin torches, and up through a trap-door in the cellars of the Hôtel de Ville, where they gave a terrible fright to a group of bibulous insurgents squatting peacefully around a fire. The alarm was sounded, but too late.

There now ensued lengthy parleys aimed at effecting a bloodless evacuation of the building, in which Dorian (the outstanding Minister of Munitions, and the one member of the Government trusted by the 'Reds') and Delescluze (who had emerged from this evening of wrangling as the 'Red' with the greatest qualities of leadership) played the principal roles. At last an agreement was reached; the Government would hold imme-diate elections and there would be no reprisals against any of the insurgents. At 3 a.m., the march-out began. Heading the procession, farcically reminiscent of guests going into a banquet, came General Tamisier, arm-in-arm with Blanqui; then came

Dorian with Delescluze, and the rest of the Government paired off each with an insurgent leader. True to form, only the slippery Pyat was absent, having – with prescience – 'disappeared' the moment the tide seemed to have turned.

As Washburne turned in that morning, he noted 'all the streets deserted and the stillness of death everywhere. What a city! One moment revolution, and the next the most profound calm!' The astonishing uprising had ended as suddenly as it had begun, and without a single casualty; it was indeed, as Flourens remarked cynically, 'Trochu's only successful military operation during the whole siege.' Alas for France, what ended in the small hours of 1 November was in one sense only a beginning. In flagrant breach of its undertaking, the Government the next day arrested twenty-two of the insurgent leaders. They included Blanqui, Millière, Vermorel, Vallès, Eudes, and even – eventually – the elusive Pyat. Flourens, too, was seized a month later, while up at the front. Sixteen battalion commanders of the National Guard were cashiered, all of whom, including Karl Marx's future son-in-law, Longuet, subsequently became Communards. Edmond Adam, the popular Prefect of Police, who had associated himself with Dorian's undertaking, promptly resigned. Dorian himself was torn with qualms of conscience: 'I make cannon,' he explained. 'If I stopped soon neither a bullet nor a cannon would be made,' and so, tearfully, he decided against resigning.

Nor were the arrests the only respect in which the Left felt it had been double-crossed. Probably in good faith, it claimed that Dorian had promised elections to replace the Provisional Government. What actually took place, on 3 November, was nothing more than a plebiscite requesting an answer of 'yes' or 'no' to a vote of confidence in the Government. The result was 560,000 to 53,000, which was regarded by the Government as a notable victory and by the 'Reds' as a manifest swindle – which indeed it was.

To the Left's existing list of grievances was now added a new bitterness that would have incalculable results when the Siege was ended. Summing up the Government's apparent display of firmness (of which he approved) young Tommy Bowles of the London *Morning Post* wrote optimistically: 'The day will have taught the Parisians one thing, that the dreaded *spectre rouge* is a very harmless turnip-headed ghost after all.'

Events were to prove him horribly wrong.

— 6 —

BY BALLOON FROM PARIS

In the unrelieved gloom that hemmed them in from every side at the beginning of November, there was just one thing that could bring a glow of pride to the hearts of all Parisians; the sight of the balloons of Paris, rising up with graceful bobs and curtsies to drift defiantly out over the enemy camp. It was the French, after all, who had invented both the gas- and the hot-air balloon; and they had even used them as early as 1793 to carry dispatches across the enemy lines. Now, a symbol of Paris's resistance, they represented her one thin lifeline with the rest of civilisation, and a great morale-booster to her own people.

When the siege began, there were only seven existing balloons in the city, some of them in shreds. The intrepid French aeronauts went to work on them, literally with paste-pot and paper, and three days after the first successful flight made by Durouf on 23 September a regular 'balloon post' was established. Among the first to send a letter by it was the eighty-six-year-old daughter of the inventor, Mlle de Montgolfier. Special light-weight forms were devised, not unlike today's air-letters – sometimes with slogans in stilted German on the exterior (just in case they fell into enemy hands): 'Crazy people, shall we always throttle each other for the pleasure and pride of kings?' or 'Paris defies her enemy! All France is rising; death to the invaders!'

After Durouf, balloons took off at a rate of about two or three a week, usually from an empty space at the foot of the Solférino Tower on top of Montmartre, or from outside the Gare du Nord and the Gare d'Orléans. Godard, one of a family of veteran aeronauts, got away successfully suspended from two small balloons lashed together and appropriately named *Les États-Unis*. Tissandier, flying in the patched-up *Céleste*, which in peacetime had never been capable of staying in the air for more than thirty-five minutes, managed to reach Dreux (fifty miles from Paris) after passing so low over Versailles that he could see Prussian soldiers sun-bathing on the lawns. Lutz, travelling aboard the *Ville de Florence*, found himself descending rapidly into the Seine, and was forced to jettison a sackful of top-secret Government dispatches. Remarkably enough, it was returned to him on landing by some peasants, and he managed to escape with them through the Prussian lines to Tours, disguised as a cowherd. Another unfortunate, faced with a similar crisis, threw his lunch pack overboard in mistake for ballast; yet a third threw himself out, but fortunately landed in a soft beet-field.

Not until the eighteenth flight, on 25 October, did a manned balloon (curiously, the *Montgolfier*) fall into Prussian hands. It does seem little less than miraculous, today, that so many of the Paris balloons succeeded in getting through. Equipment was incredibly primitive. The balloons themselves were constructed simply of varnished cotton, because silk was unobtainable, and filled with highly explosive coal-gas; thus they were exceptionally vulnerable to Prussian sharp-shooters. Capable of unpredictable motion in all three dimensions, none of which was controllable, in inexperienced hands they had an unpleasant habit of shooting suddenly up to six thousand feet, then falling back again almost to ground-level. Huddled in their draughty baskets, the balloonists suffered agonisingly from the cold as the winter grew more bitter. Often they carried no compass, and after a few minutes of twisting, giddy progress they had in any case lost all sense of direction. To every corner of France – and beyond – the winds blew them, and they seldom had the remotest idea where they were on landing.

> '*Audace humaine! effort du captif! sainte rage!*
> *Effraction enfin, plus forte que la cage!*

Queuing for food at a grocery, 1870

A barricade during the Commune, 1871

Destruction of the Vendôme Column during the Commune, 1871

The Tuileries burned by the Communards

Défense de la Commune

RÉPUBLIQUE.FRANÇAISE

PEUPLES NOTRE EXEMPLE

SERA SUIVI!!!

Personification of the French Republic
as Louise Michel tramples on the heads of
Louis Adolphe Thiers and Napoleon III

Que faut-il à cet être, atome au large front,
Pour vaincre ce qui n'a ni fin, ni bord, ni fond,
Pour dompter le vent, trombe, et l'écume, avalanche?
Dans le ciel une toile et sur mer une planche.'

So wrote Hugo in praise of these early cosmonauts. Yet, for all the perils, there was never any shortage of recruits. The sense of exhilaration – the joys of popping champagne corks in those precarious baskets to toast 'Death to the invaders! *Vive la France!'* as the balloonists escaped over the Prussian lines – diminished any sensation of fear.

In the deserted halls of the Paris railway stations, assembly lines were set up for fabricating balloons. Between the rusted lines, the completed balloons were varnished, stretched out, partially inflated, like rows of massive whales. In the waiting-rooms, sailors were busy braiding halliards. From the station girders, 'dummy' baskets were suspended for training new recruits.

Meanwhile the best brains in Paris sought frenetically for an invention whereby the balloons could also be flown *back* into Paris. For, being unsteerable, they afforded only a one-sided means of communication. Ideas proliferated: a huge 'dirigible' to be propelled by a 400 horsepower engine; sails, oars, rockets and even the harnessing of ten thousand pigeons. Rumours ran round that a team of mighty eagles from the zoo had actually been harnessed to a balloon, 'guided by an aeronaut by means of a piece of raw flesh fastened to the end of a long stick'. One balloon did leave Paris with a propeller hand-driven by three beefy sailors; but it still flew in the wrong direction. An expert balloonist, Tissandier, persistently attempted the return flight. But none succeeded.

The humble carrier-pigeon was to prove the only means of breaking the blockade in reverse. In the first recorded usage of micro-photography, Government despatches in Tours were reduced to minute size and rolled into a pellicle, so that one pigeon could carry up to 40,000 dispatches. On reaching Paris, these were then projected by magic lantern and transcribed by a battery of clerks. In the course of the siege, 392 birds were sent off, of which 59 actually reached Paris. The remainder were taken by birds of prey, died of cold and hunger, or ended in Prussian pies. Their safe arrival had a signal effect on Parisian spirits, and when the war ended there was serious talk of rewarding the noble birds, which some compared to the geese of Rome, by incorporating them in the city coat of arms.

The Prussians began to take the balloons seriously. Attempts to send up sharp-shooters in rival balloons ended in disaster. Herr Krupp was instructed to design a special anti-balloon cannon, but that too proved ineffective. The most dangerous challenge to the balloonists was provided by the Prussians' excellent telegraph system, which tracked the balloons and sent Uhlan patrols after them. The counter-measures began to bear fruit. First, the *Montgolfier* was seized on landing in Alsace after a three-hundred-mile flight. Two days later the *Vauban* carrying Reitlinger, a special emissary of Jules Favre, descended in a forest near Verdun, and Reitlinger only reached the Belgian frontier after the narrowest of escapes from Uhlan patrols. That same day the *Normandie* also came down near Verdun and was seized by Uhlans.

Now the Parisians became forced to send up balloons by night, which resulted in some of the grimmest and most dramatic flights of the siege. After taking off at 1 a.m. on 25 November, the *Archimède* came down at dawn in Holland and would undoubtedly have been blown out to sea had its flight lasted a few minutes longer. In December the *Ville de Paris* landed at Wetzlar in Germany, believing it to be Belgium; and five days later the *Chanzy* ended up in Bavaria after an eight-hour flight. But no flight was more perilous or more remarkable than that of the *Ville d'Orléans*, which, after a terrifying flight of fifteen hours, landed in the middle of Norway – nine hundred miles away – to the total astonishment of its crew!

By a real miracle, until 28 November and the thirty-fourth balloon, the *Jacquard*, there had not been one single fatality. Manned by a young sailor called Prince, the *Jacquard* was spotted from the Lizard lighthouse, disappearing out into the Atlantic.

Altogether some 65 manned balloons left Paris during the Siege. They carried 164 passengers, 381 pigeons, five dogs, and nearly eleven tons of official dispatches, including approximately two and a half million letters. Six landed in Belgium, four in Holland, two in Germany, one in Norway, two were lost at sea, but only five fell into enemy hands. It was an epic achievement, by any standard.

The balloon was not the only scientific development to occupy fertile Parisian minds. Inventions and ideas of all kinds, many produced in the fervid atmosphere of the 'Red' Clubs, poured into the Government. One suggested poisoning the Seine where it left Paris; another, unleashing the more ferocious beasts in the zoo on the Prussians; a third proposed a 'musical *mitrailleuse*' which, siren-like, would lure the *Kultur*-lovers by playing Beethoven and Schubert, then scythe them down. Slightly more prophetically practical ideas included a 'mobile rampart', a precursor of the tank; shells that would emit 'suffocating vapours'; and 'pockets of Satan', filled with petroleum, which would burst over enemy positions, covering them with a blanket of napalm-like fire.

Of all the emanations from the Clubs, none was more exotic than Jules Allix's '*doigts prussiques*', pins dipped (appropriately) in prussic acid, with which the women of Paris were to defend their honour. These were to be the weapon of a remarkable corps created by Felix Belly, called the 'Amazons of the Seine'. 'The Prussian advances towards you – you put forth your hand,' explained Allix, 'you prick him – he is dead, and you are pure and tranquil.' Alas, the 'Amazons' were never put to the test. It all appears to have been something of a confidence trick; having pocketed numerous enrolment fees, Belly disappeared. (Allix later held an appointment under the Commune, and ended in a lunatic asylum.)

Meanwhile, all over Paris, under Dorian's inspired guidance, the more humdrum weapons and munitions were being turned out in vast new plants or tiny basement rooms. By the end of the siege, Dorian's workshops had produced no less than four hundred cannon. Half of them had been financed by popular

— 7 —

THE GREAT SORTIE

With the 'Red' leaders in gaol, awaiting a possible death sentence, the greatest danger confronting Trochu's conduct of the war – that of a revolution inside Paris – seemed to have been averted. Belleville was sullenly in check; but for how long? Yet, as November arrived and the Siege approached the end of its second month, neutrals inside Paris sensed a distinct plunge in morale. On 6 November Labouchere reported: 'I never remember to have witnessed a day of such general gloom since the commencement of the Siege. The feeling of despair is, I hear, still stronger in the army.' More serious still was the grim news that milk had run out; and on the 16th Washburne reported to the State Department: 'Fresh meat is getting almost out of the question. . . . They have begun on dogs, cats, and rats. . . . The gas is also giving out.'

All this, coming so soon after the shock of 31 October's events, made even Trochu realise that something had to be done swiftly and dramatically. The time had come for a major military effort. But where, and how? After lengthy deliberations, Trochu and Ducrot came to settle for a carefully planned break-out effort that would be made to the west of Paris, aiming for the port of Le Havre.

Suddenly in the midst of their councils-of-war, however, on 14 November a miraculous piece of news reached Paris via a French line-crosser. Gambetta's newly created armies, under the command of General d'Aurelle de Paladines, had five days previously inflicted a great defeat upon the Bavarian General von der Tann at Coulmiers. In this first genuine victory of the

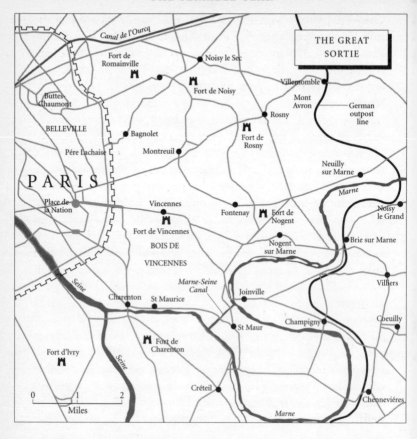

war, Orleans itself had been recaptured, and the enemy seemed to be reeling back in full retreat. Paris exploded in a delirium of joy. 'We have passed from the lowest depths of despair to the wildest confidence,' exclaimed Labouchere. 'I am so happy,' declared Juliette Lambert, 'that I would willingly give myself up to arrogance. Yes, we have a success.' Strangers kissed each other on the boulevard. Trochu now ordered Ducrot to accelerate his break-out plans with all vigour, so as to link up with the advancing d'Aurelle.

But, because of the tenuous, one-sided state of communications with Paris, a disastrous misunderstanding now occurred.

Gambetta, heady with success, decided that *he* should call the tune; he would advance on Paris via Orleans – that is, from the *south* – and Ducrot would have to conform to his plans. Rationally, apart from the fact that overall command of the armies still rested in Paris, it should have been the other way round, because the limitations of the balloon service made it much easier for Ducrot to tell Gambetta what he was doing, rather than *vice versa*.

Meanwhile, Ducrot was continuing with preparations for thrusting every available man and gun out of Paris towards the *west*. Then, on 18 November, a pigeon was received from Gambetta urging Trochu to co-operate by striking southwards. The next day a shocked and fuming Ducrot was told that his offensive would now have to be transported, lock stock, and barrel to the other side of Paris. It was no mean undertaking to shift 400 guns, 54 pontoons and 80,000 men with all their supplies and equipment through the Paris streets.

Worse still, the change of direction would involve some complicated bridging operations across the Marne, in face of the enemy. And, instead of the weeks Ducrot had had to lay his plans for the sortie to the west, now there was only a matter of days to complete preparations. It was impossible, too, to hide these massive troop movements from the Prussians (they were indeed freely discussed on the streets of Paris), and several days before the attack began Moltke was reinforcing his units on the threatened sector.

The date chosen for the 'Great Sortie' was 29 November. But for several days Trochu procrastinated before informing Gambetta, and it was not until the 24th – five days only before D-Day – that a message was finally sent off. As France's extraordinarily bad luck would have it, that crucial message was entrusted to the *Ville d'Orléans* – the balloon that made the incredible flight to Norway by mistake. Thus Gambetta was never informed when, or where, the break-out attempt was going to take place until it was too late.

Tense expectation and a new sense of urgency filled Paris in these last days before the 'Great Sortie', and nowhere more so than among the National Guard. Under pressure of the repeated demands that the Guard participate in actual fighting, culminating in the outbreak of 31 October, the Government had yielded to the extent of forming special *Compagnies de Guerre* of the youngest and fittest which would march with the regulars.

'A tremendous battle is expected day after day,' Edwin Child, now a volunteer Guardsman, wrote to his mother. 'There will be more than 200,000 men engaged on the French side . . . 100,000 men have been selected from out of the National Guard, armed and fully equipped for war, and a finer set of men it would be difficult to find . . .'

On the night of 28 November, awoken by an immense cannonade which even out at Versailles had deprived an anxious King of Prussia of his sleep, Goncourt climbed up to the roof of his building. There, in a 'night without stars', he saw 'a succession of small dots of fire that flicker up like gas-jets, followed by sonorous echoes. These great voices of death in the midst of the silence of the night stir one. After some time, the howling of dogs joins in with the thunder of the cannon; frightened voices of awoken humans begin whispering . . . my ear, straining out of the window, can hear nothing more than the cannonade in the distance, far in the distance, resembling the dull noise that an oar makes when it strikes the side of a boat.'

Behind the scenes, all was far from well as the 'Great Sortie' began. Heavy rain had swollen the Marne where Ducrot intended to make his main crossing, and the pontoons were swept away. In despair, Ducrot contemplated scrapping the whole operation. But Trochu persuaded him that it was unthinkable. Apart from anything else, the danger of revolt by a disappointed mob was too great. So he would concentrate on the subsidiary actions at Champigny and Bry, and postpone the main attack in the centre by twenty-four hours.

The first news to be posted up outside the Hôtel de Ville was encouraging to the Parisians: 'All General Ducrot's divisions have crossed the Marne!' As usual, Paris fastened on this early glimmer, building out of it a resounding victory. Bourse prices ran up their biggest gains since September.

Ducrot had in fact managed to throw bridgeheads across the Marne at both Champigny and Bry, and under a tremendous barrage from Fort Nogent his troops captured these two towns during the morning of the 29th. It was when they surmounted the steep Villiers escarpment above that they first ran into serious trouble. From positions carefully prepared behind stone park walls, Moltke's Württembergers directed a murderous rifle-fire on the attackers. Casualties reached almost 1914 proportions; one regiment lost its colonel and four hundred men.

Elsewhere, Tommy Bowles was able to observe a course of events that was typical of the battle as a whole that day. The 170th (Belleville) Battalion of the National Guard was at the front for the first time: 'Over the Marne I could see the red trousers swarming up the hills beyond Champigny, and the artillery alternatively galloping up and firing, while the Prussian line had already – this was eleven o'clock – disappeared over the crest.'

The prospects looked favourable, but half-an-hour later Bowles was reporting that the action 'seemed to warm, and some of the French skirmishers began to fall back – in very good order, however – firing and turning slowly. Wounded men, pale and bloody, now began to arrive, some born on *brancards*.'

Moving up to a captured Prussian barricade, Bowles was then met 'by a crowd of breathless men swarming around and through it, and running to the shelter of a wall on the right of the road. . . . The Belleville Battalion was there, and their remarks were not calculated to inspire confidence in their courage. "*Nous sommes battus*," they said, looking with pale faces at one another, while some of them silently left the ranks, and walked with a careless air towards the rear . . . I saw that the fortune of battle had, indeed, distinctly turned. The French were now running fast back over the crest of the hill. . . . It was now half-past twelve. I returned to the Place in the centre of the village . . . a seething mob of soldiers of all arms struggled and wrestled to get through the village, without order, without leaders, without any idea what to do or whither to go, unless it were to avoid the Prussians. . . . They fought with each other . . . and trampled even on their wounded comrades, whom the first comers had avoided. It was not an army that was retreating, it was not even a respectable mob.'

Riding about the front with utter fearlessness on a magnificent white charger, pushing defaulters back into the line at the point of his sabre, Ducrot watched the assaults on the Villiers plateau bog down. The various diversionary efforts on other parts of the front had also ended in costly failures. By the end of the first day, the French had lost 5,236 men, the Germans 2,091. Because of the traditional inadequacy of the French *ambulances*, there were some terrible scenes of suffering among the wounded. All day they streamed back before the eyes of the shocked Parisians, their faces bearing (said Goncourt) 'the horrible anxiety of their wounds, the uncertainty of amputation, the uncertainty of life or death'.

On 1 December a twenty-four-hour truce to remove the wounded was requested, and granted. The next day the Prussians launched a massive counter-attack. On the road to Champigny Ducrot was met by 'an avalanche of vehicles, infantry-men, cavalry, all descending at full speed towards the Marne'. Nothing could prevent their rout. The following day, Ducrot's army withdrew across the Marne, under cover of a merciful fog. The Great Sortie had failed.

The news was not released in Paris until the 5th. There was a cold silence over the city. Goncourt spoke for all Parisians when he entered in his journal: 'the heights and depths of hope; this is what kills one. One believes oneself saved. Then one realises one is lost. . . . To day the recrossing of the Marne by Ducrot has thrown us back into the darkness of failure and despair.'

That same day yet another grievous blow descended. It came in the form of a letter from Moltke, addressed to Trochu, studiously polite, but informing him of a crushing defeat inflicted upon Gambetta, resulting in the recapture of Orleans. The Great Sortie had cost 12,000 officers and men; it had failed, and at the same time the relieving army from Tours had been stopped in its tracks. The plight of Paris now seemed hopeless. But still the fear of 'Red' revolution, combined with the revealed harshness of Prussian peace terms, purged any idea of capitulation from the minds of the Government. The Siege would go on, though since the supreme military effort had failed it would henceforth be merely a matter of survival and attrition.

— 8 —

HUNGER

The disaster on the Marne was not long past before Parisian minds became preoccupied with other, far more grimly immediate topics than purely military considerations. On 8 December, Goncourt noted in his journal: 'People are talking only of what they eat, what they can eat, and what there is to eat. Conversation consists of this, and nothing more. . . . Hunger begins and famine is on the horizon.' He found Théophile Gautier lamenting 'that he has to wear braces for the first time, his abdomen no longer supporting his trousers'.

Cheese, butter and milk, were now little more than memories of the past, and the vast herds of cattle and sheep that filled the Bois in September had now vanished. Fresh vegetables had run out; for one franc a day, and at considerable risk to themselves, 'marauders' were sent out under the protection of *Mobiles* to grub about in 'no-man's-land'.

Early in October smart Paris had begun to eat horsemeat, first introduced by Parisian butchers four years previously as a cheap provender for the poor. To a *belle* who (exceptionally) had refused to dine with him, a frustrated Victor Hugo wrote:

> *Je vous aurais offert un repas sans rival:*
> *J'aurais tué Pegase et je l'aurais fait cuire,*
> *Afin de vous servir une aile de cheval.'*

Many a superb champion of the turf, including two trotting horses presented by the Tsar to Louis-Napoleon at the Great

46

Exhibition, ended its days in the casserole, but by mid-November these supplies too had become exhausted.

Now the signs 'Feline and Canine Butchers' made their début. As more and more of the two traditional domestic enemies became reconciled in the cooking-pot, Gautier claimed that they seemed to grow instinctively aware of their peril: 'Soon the animals observed that man was regarding them in a strange manner and that, under the pretext of caressing them, his hand was feeling them like the fingers of a butcher, to ascertain the state of their *embonpoint*. More intellectual and more suspicious than dogs, the cats were the first to understand, and adopted the greatest prudence in their relations.'

Next it was the turn of the rats. Although – together with the carrier-pigeon – the rat was to become the most fabled animal of the Siege, and from December on a good rat-hunt was one of the favourite pastimes of the National Guard, the number actually consumed was relatively few. (According to one contemporary American calculation although on what it was based is not revealed, only 300 rats were eaten during the whole Siege, compared with 65,000 horses, 5,000 cats, and 1,200 dogs.) Because of the lavish sauces required to make them palatable, they were essentially a rich man's dish; hence the famous menus of the Jockey Club, featuring such delicacies as *salmi de rats*.

Then the hard-pressed butchers turned their eyes to the zoos. Because of the danger involved in killing them, the lions and tigers survived, as did the monkeys, protected apparently by the Darwinian instincts of the Parisians, and the hippopotamus from the Jardin des Plantes, for whose vast live-weight no butcher could afford the reserve price of 80,000 francs. Otherwise no animal was exempt. By the end of December, even the pride of the Jardin d'Acclimatation, two elephants called Castor and Pollux, were dispatched after several disgracefully inept attempts with dum-dum bullets. Their trunks, a special delicacy, were sold to wealthy Parisians for 40 francs a pound. By the first days of January, Bowles was recording: 'I have now dined off camel, antelope, dog, donkey, mule and elephant, which I approve in the order in which I have written.'

At first, the irrepressible Parisian sense of humour was provided with a rich source of jokes by these bizarre menus (for those who could afford them). *Le Figaro* related how a man was pursued through Paris by a pack of dogs, barking loudly at his heels; he could not understand their interest, until he recalled that he had eaten a rat for breakfast. After a dog dinner, one of the Goncourt's circle was heard to comment: 'next they'll be serving us the shepherd!' In fact the Parisians were never quite reduced to cannibalism.

But it was hardly a joke for the poor who could no longer afford the astronomic prices of the bare essentials of life. Despite the quite sensible entreaties of Blanqui and the Left wing, no effort was made by the Government to establish proper control of food distribution until too late. Then the measures were ineffectual and inequitable; virtually the only effective rationing was achieved by that most unfair of all criteria – by price.

There were black marketeers running every kind of racket, and many of the affluent had their own private supplies. One British banker living in Paris wrote home on 17 November: 'Paris can stand out for two months more . . . I have still fresh meat of the cow I killed, for breakfast, and milk and butter from the one still living . . . we dine well at the Jockey Club. In fine we get enough, and people do not complain.' Meanwhile, hour after hour, the wretched housewives waited, often from 3 a.m. onwards, often leaving empty-handed, with hatred in their hearts for the *petit bourgeois* as represented by the heartless butcher, and for the rich bourgeois who could afford to buy without queuing.

For those with even a little money, the situation during the Siege was rarely worse than it was for the average Briton in the direst moments of the U-boat blockade in the First World War. But for the really poor, though few were actually to die of starvation, it was seldom more than an arm's length away, and more and more found common cause with the 'Reds' in their grievances against the inequities of life.

Perhaps it was undernourishment, as much as any other factor, which kept the 'Reds' passive throughout the whole of December, and into January. But in the meantime boredom, depression and lethargy reached new heights.

'Nothing crueller,' wrote Goncourt, 'than to live in obscurity, in the night, in complete ignorance of the tragedy that threatens you.'

By mid-December, Labouchere sensed that 'a dead, apathetic torpor has settled over the town'. It was having its effect on the Army. Slackness and absenteeism were on the increase. Something had to be undertaken to restore morale. Now, once again, came tantalising news from the outside world that a new Gambetta army – this time under Faidherbe, approaching from the north – was on its way to help Paris. Though now deeply committed to pessimism, Ducrot decided to attempt another sortie; striking for a second time in the direction of Le Bourget.

Alas, it was the story of the Great Sortie repeated. Aware in advance of Parisian intentions, Moltke had reinforcements waiting to mow down the French attackers. And then the thermometer suddenly plunged to a level rarely experienced in France. Soldiers froze to death in their foxholes on the Le Bourget steppe. To Ducrot the plight of his retreating troops 'made one pity to see them . . . heads wound about with scarves, their blankets folded and refolded round their bodies, legs enveloped in rags . . .' They no longer resembled soldiers; it was, said Ducrot, 'Moscow at the gates of Paris'.

Faidherbe too was driven back, and after this second battle of Le Bourget Ducrot admitted, 'Hope of forcing the lines of investment abandoned even the most intrepid hearts.' Finally, on 22 December, Trochu was forced to send to Tours a balloon message warning that Paris would have no rations after 20 January. What small elements of comedy there had once existed in the Siege were vanishing, an undilutedly tragic key taking their place.

9

BOMBARD PARIS!

As conditions worsened in Paris, the defenders must often have gazed across at the Prussian Camp with mixed curiosity and envy. How much better things doubtless were for the besieging force! Indeed, on the few occasions when Trochu's men captured an enemy redoubt, it was depressing to discover just how solidly and how comfortably the invader had installed himself. In the open country, the Prussians had dug deep shelters in the shape of a cone. At the centre of the cone was a large fire, around which, in cold weather, the troops slept, their heads pointing outwards. These were sharply in contrast with the miserable, wet, cold and exposed positions generally inhabited by the besieged.

In the Prussian fortifications life was reasonably agreeable and secure. Occasionally nightfall brought an unpleasant shock when someone infringed the strict blackout precautions; but otherwise French shell-fire did little to upset the leisurely routine of life. Out of the line, the Prussians spent their time pleasantly enough, rowing on the lake at Enghien or skating when winter set in, or just goggling at the wonders of Versailles. There was no shortage of food of all kinds, and excellent wine 'liberated' from French cellars was also plentiful.

Despite this looting of cellars, however – the prerogative of the conqueror everywhere – gratuitous vandalism was not excessive. When the Siberian cold of December struck, doors, furniture, panelling, and sometimes even grand pianos were smashed up for firewood. This was, however, a common necessity of war, in which – as many an absentee French householder discovered to his sorrow after the Siege – his own side was by no means retrograde.

Nobody did himself better than Bismarck, ensconced with the Prussian Court at Versailles. At lunch, when the French were down to their last elephant, and facing a Christmas with empty larders, the gluttonous Chancellor is recorded as grumbling: 'There is always a dish too much. I had already decided to ruin my stomach with goose and olives, and here is Reinfeld ham of which I cannot help taking too much, merely because I want to get my own share. . . . And here is Varzin wild boar, too!'

To a casual visitor, life at Versailles gave the appearance of calm monotony. But beneath the surface, all was far from calm. First of all there was the over-riding political problem of German unity, closer to Bismarck's heart than any other issue. Assiduously he had been engineering behind the scenes to get all the German states to agree to cap the triumph over France by promoting the King of Prussia to be Emperor of all Germans. The worry was causing his varicose veins to pain him. Then there were heated arguments with Moltke and the generals as to how much of France should be grabbed by way of war reparations. Somehow at Versailles the spirit of the court of Louis XV, its intrigues and jealousies, had infected those stolid Teutons. There was constant bickering between princelings over promotion, and bitter divisions had also arisen over the conduct of the war, as it had dragged on and on beyond the capitulation at Sedan.

Both the King and his son, the Crown Prince, were repeatedly in a state of pessimism. 'It looks more and more' wrote the Crown Prince on 16 December, when Faidherbe was active round Amiens, 'as though our military situation is once more to become critical . . . His Majesty's outlook on the immediate future is of the blackest.' The recuperative powers of the French, as demonstrated by Gambetta, repeatedly dismayed him; 'It is positively amazing how quickly, after an Army has been beaten and put to flight, ever fresh masses of men are again got together and armed, which in their turn fight well.' A particular fear gnawing at the Prussian leaders, right to the end, was that Gambetta might sever the tenuous line linking the siege army with its rear, across the Rhine. What encouragement Gambetta and Trochu would have received, had they been able to observe these uncertainties in the Prussian camp!

In the bitter cold of December, the Prussians also began to suffer. The funeral ceremonies at Versailles became increasingly frequent, noted W. H. Russell of *The Times*, as more and more of the German wounded succumbed. By January, the sick list had reached thirty to forty men per company, and sometimes higher. Accordingly, morale showed an alarming decline too, while drunkenness was becoming a problem. To Russell on New Year's Eve, the Crown Prince 'expressed the utmost weariness of the war, because it was useless expenditure of blood and prolonging of misery and suffering to all'. Even Bismarck was prone to depression, confiding to his wife: 'The men are freezing and falling sick; the war is dragging out; the neutrals are interfering in our affairs . . . and France is arming.' Time no longer seemed to be on the Prussian side. The Crown Prince predicted sombrely: 'The longer this struggle lasts, the better for the enemy and the worse for us. The public opinion of Europe has not remained unaffected by the spectacle. We are no longer looked upon as the innocent sufferers of wrong, but rather as the arrogant victors, no longer content with the conquest of the foe, but fain to bring about his utter ruin.'

Clearly the war had to be brought rapidly to an end. But how? There was only one way: bombard Paris into submission!

The generals had been urging this course of action for many weeks. Moltke, on purely military grounds, was hesitant. The Crown Prince was strongly opposed, for humanitarian reasons: 'I pass sleepless nights when I think of the women and children,' he confided to Russell. Finally, mounting pressure at home to end the war swung over Moltke and Bismarck, and the Crown Prince was overruled.

On the morning of 27 December, a French colonel and his wife were quietly giving a breakfast party for friends at Fort Avron to the east of Paris. Suddenly the party was broken up by a heavy Prussian shell which burst without warning in the room. Six of the breakfasters were killed outright, the host and hostess gravely wounded. Ceaselessly during the next two days Prussian guns of a calibre hitherto unknown continued to plunge their huge shells down on Avron, until the whole locality had become 'literally shaven'.

The artillerymen at Versailles were delighted by the unqualified success of what had been regarded as a 'dummy run'. It did seem indeed possible to smash Paris herself into submission. Next the southern forts had to be silenced, in order that the heavy guns could move closer to bombard the city. For a week shells rained down on the forts.

Then, on 5 January the bombardment of Paris proper began; in the coldly technical words of Moltke, 'an elevation of 30 degrees, by a peculiar contrivance, sent the shot into the heart of the city'. What was probably the first shell burst in the Rue Lalande on the Left Bank, scattering its fragments over a baby asleep in its cradle. Other great masses of iron furrowed up the Montparnasse Cemetery, whose occupants were beyond harm, but one which fell near the Luxembourg literally sliced in two a little girl on her way home from school. Tragedy followed on tragedy.

'The shells have begun falling in the Rue Boileau,' wrote Goncourt on the 6th. 'Tomorrow, no doubt, they will be falling here; and even if they do not kill me, they will destroy everything I still love in life.' They were falling at a rate of three to four hundred a day. The domes of the Panthéon and the Invalides became favourite targets, and the areas around them suffered the most heavily. The Salpetrière Hospital, a prominent building with a large Red Cross on its roof and 2,000 aged women and 1,000 lunatics, was hit repeatedly, giving rise to the suspicion that the Prussians were deliberately firing on hospitals. The Odéon Theatre, also in use as a temporary hospital, was hit twice, and other shells damaged the beautiful church of St Sulpice off the Boulevard St-Germain.

A mass migration of fugitives from the Left Bank now began, comparable to what was to become a common spectacle under another German onslaught, seventy years later. But after the initial fear of the unknown had passed, indignation became the principal reaction to the bombardment; indignation that reached a climax on 11 January with the solemn funeral of six small children, killed by the same shell. It was the defilement of the *ville lumière*, the holy city, as much as the random disembowelling of innocent children or the shelling of hospitals that outraged most Parisians, while the affront to humanitarian principles earned France stronger support abroad than at any other time during the war.

In turn, as relief grew at the relatively little damage and casualties caused, indignation gave way to a remarkable indifference to the bombardment. Already by 8 January, Washburne could write: 'The carelessness and nonchalance of the Parisians in all this business is wonderful . . . Ladies and gentlemen now make excursions to the Point du Jour to see the shells fall' while small boys made a killing in the sale of shell-fragment souvenirs. 'There is no panic or alarm,' noted Goncourt on the 9th. 'Everybody seems to be leading his usual life, and the café proprietors, with admirable sang-froid, are replacing the mirrors shattered by the blast of exploding shells.'

The bombardment was proving a failure. Monsters as the Krupp siege guns were by nineteenth-century standards, they were inadequate to the task. When the final reckoning came to be made, it was found that in the three weeks the shelling of Paris lasted only 97 people were actually killed and 278 wounded, with 1,400 buildings damaged for an expenditure of 12,000 shells; while the Prussians themselves lost several hundred gunners to French counter-battery fire. If anything, thought Washburne, the bombardment 'had made the people more firm and determined'.

At Versailles, however, the disappointment of realising that Moltke's bombardment was not going to bring Paris to her knees was temporarily eclipsed by an event of immense historical moment. In the Hall of Mirrors, where only a few years ago Queen Victoria had danced with Louis-Napoleon amid all the splendours of the Second Empire, belonging to that great palace bearing the inscription '*à toutes les Gloires de la France*', King Wilhelm I of Prussia was proclaimed Kaiser of the Germans. At last Bismarck had had his way. But, to the injury of the bombardment of Paris, an appalling insult had been added, one which would have to be wiped out in blood in less than half-a-century's time.

10

PARIS BREAKS

January added a new dimension to the sufferings of Paris; worse than the bombardment, and one which was greatly exacerbated by malnutrition. The cold! Fuel was now running desperately short. Already by the third week of November coal-gas, required in large quantities for the balloon service, had been stringently rationed and the streets of the *ville lumière* plunged into total darkness. Now, as if even the elements had deserted the Parisian cause, since the savage freeze-up in mid-December Paris was gripped by the bitterest winter in living memory. 'We might be able to rattle a four-in-hand across the Seine,' wrote an Irishman in Paris; 'that is, if we had not eaten the team in advance.' With coal gone, wood was rapidly running out, and there were no horses to transport what little remained.

As in every privation, once again it was the poor who suffered most acutely. A visitor to Belleville shortly after Christmas was shocked to discover that 'scarcely a vestige remained of the young saplings that peopled this outer line of boulevards, except here and there a stump with the bars of the iron fence that protected the tree lying wrenched and twisted on the soil. Farther on, huge trunks lay prostrate, around which swarmed an eager crowd of women and children, hacking with their puny hatchets at the twigs and bark'.

Soon, when their own neighbourhood had been denuded, the frantic fuel-scavengers from the east end began to descend on the more fashionable parts of Paris. On the Champs Elysées itself, Goncourt watched 'a cloud of children, armed with hatchets, knives, anything that would cut, slashing off pieces of bark with which they filled their hands, their pockets, their pinafores, while in the hole left by the felled tree, one could see the heads of old women, engaged in digging up with picks all that remained of the roots'. Meanwhile, in a contrast so typical of the Siege, at a nearby café there were 'seven or eight young *Mobile* officers, parading and coquetting around a *lorette*, deciding on a menu of fantasy and intellectual imagination for dinner'.

Clothing too was running short. In one of their many acts of charity during the Siege, the Rothschilds supplied the poor with clothes for some 48,000 children and a similar number of adults. But all this was a drop in the ocean. Shirts of newspaper began to make their appearance, with the Paris press itself boasting that such garments could 'be worn a consecutive month without ceasing to be comfortable!'

Meanwhile, hand in hand with hunger and cold, disease was also on the rise. There had been a sharp increase in deaths from smallpox and typhoid, but worst of all was the number caused by respiratory ailments (principally pneumonia), which soared from 170 during the tenth week of the siege to 1,084 by the week of 14–21 January. The mortality rate was particularly high among the children of the under-privileged. In Belleville, the spectacle of small coffins being trundled by hand to the common grave at Père Lachaise Cemetery was becoming depressingly commonplace. Those who could yet afford to dine out were repeatedly shocked by the pinched and wan faces of children begging at the doors of restaurants.

Calling on the house of an absent friend, Labouchère found 'three families installed in it – one family, consisting of a father, a mother, and three children, were boiling a piece of horse meat about four inches square, in a bucket full of water. This exceedingly thin soup was to last them for three days. The day before they had each had a carrot.' On 7 January Goncourt with his usual aptness summed up the outlook of a dying city: 'The sufferings of Paris during the Siege? A joke for two months. In the third month the joke went sour. Now nobody finds it funny any more, and we are moving fast towards starvation.'

The prospects now seemed so hopeless that the pious Trochu had taken to praying publicly for a miracle to the city's patron saint, St Geneviève, whose intercession had repulsed the Huns from the gates of Paris just fourteen centuries earlier. Trochu and a majority of the Government felt that the city should hold out as long as the food lasted, and make one last major attempt at a sortie. It was not, however, until 15 January that the possibility of surrender was actually mentioned at a Cabinet session. Then, as on the eve of the Great Sortie at the end of November, not military considerations – nor even the problem of food – precipitated a fateful decision. As Ducrot was to remark on the Siege in retrospect, 'virtually the whole defence revolved around a single thing! *Fear of a rebellion*. . . . One was constantly obliged to face two enemies: one which, night and day, tightened his ring of fire and steel, the other which at every instant was awaiting the moment to hurl itself upon the Hôtel de Ville.' Upon the first suggestion that the city should now surrender, one doubt immediately presented itself to all minds; would the 'Reds' permit a surrender?

Up at Belleville, angry voices were once again reaching a new pitch. Louder than ever were demands for a *sortie torrentielle* of the citizenry of Paris – of the National Guard. These demands were backed up by red-dyed posters that surreptitiously appeared all over Paris on 6 January. Drafted by Delescluze and signed by 'The Delegates of the Twenty Arrondissements', these called for the Government to be instantly replaced by the mystical Commune, and – once again – for the immediate employment in battle of the National Guard.

That the proletarian population of Paris after all its deprivations should still be so ardent for battle was astonishing. But it was unmistakable. At the same time, among the bourgeoisie the slogan, 'Rather Bismarck than Blanqui', heard with increasing regularity, was indicative of increasing war-weariness. Even out at Versailles the Prussians seemed to be aware of the gulf opening among the besieged; on 16 January, General von Blumenthal noted: 'It looks as though in Paris a catastrophe were about to happen to the present rulers there.'

That same day, aware of its dangerous predicament, Trochu's Government took a desperate and cynical decision, after one of its members had remarked brutally: 'When there are 10,000 National Guards lying on the ground, opinion will calm down.' Accordingly, plans were laid for hurling the National Guard into a last sortie, towards Buzenval in the sector nearest to Versailles; needless to say, the sector most strongly defended by the Prussians.

In the National Guard, boredom, drunkenness and alcoholism had reached new depths. There had been altogether too many false alarms; too many occasions when Guard battalions had been called out for an alert, made to stand around for up to eight hours in the biting cold, then dismissed. During one such alert the day before Christmas Eve as Edwin Child entered typically in his diary: 'We were not wanted during the day so about 6 returned to our quarters, made up a good fire and tried to sleep but found it impossible the cold being too intense, in spite of our blankets and capotes, so smoked away the night.' Later, to keep themselves amused, he and his comrades demolished a wooden railway station for fuel. By 12 January, he was ruminating gloomily: 'Wonder whether I shall see the end, or leave my carcase to rot in the field of battle, cannot say that I much care which way it is, but would like to stick a Prussian before the latter arrives.'

The whole disastrous story of the National Guard during the Siege was a shining example of half-measures. In response to popular pressures, the Government had raised 400,000 *Gardes*; but, doubtful of their reliability (both military and political), it had trained and armed them insufficiently to be of any combat value – yet just enough to constitute the most potent revolutionary threat the nineteenth century had yet seen.

For all the torpor that futility had induced, the National Guard responded with tragic enthusiasm to the opportunity the Government was at last offering it. On 18 January, it began its approach march to the west of Paris, ready to attack the world's most efficient professional army. 'It was' thought Goncourt, 'a grandiose, soul-stirring sight that army marching towards the guns booming in the distance, an army with, in its midst, grey-bearded civilians who were fathers, beardless youngsters who were sons, and in its open ranks women carrying their husband's or their lover's rifle slung across their backs.'

But by afternoon on the first day of the operation, the Prussian guns had checked the attack all along the line. As before, Ducrot was there, conspicuously mounted on his white charger, well ahead of his troops, and preserved as if by magic; but once again his temerity could do nothing to alter the course of the battle. Although there were instances when the French – including the *Garde* – fought with outstanding courage, Bowles witnessed a disquieting occurrence that day when National Guards were supposed to be backing up a regiment of *Mobiles*: 'very pretty they looked, coming up the hill at a run, with fixed bayonets, the colonel puffing heavily in front, and the aide-de-camp brandishing his sabre and cheering them on. When they got a little below me, however, and began to hear the balls singing past their heads, they ducked to a man, with unanimity that was positively comic, slackened speed, stopped by common consent, and then falling flat on their stomachs, opened fire to the front on the *Mobiles*!'

As darkness fell, Trochu's own party was also fired on by some disorientated National Guards. The next morning he gave the orders to withdraw from Buzenval. The final sortie had failed. It was more than the tenuous threads of discipline could withstand. Wrote Ducrot: 'Hardly was the word retreat pronounced than in the rear areas on the left the débâcle began . . . everything broke up, everything went. . . . On the roads the muddle was terrifying . . . across the open country the National Guards were taking to their heels in every direction. . . . Soldiers, wandering, lost, searched for their company, their officers.' As the National Guard streamed through the streets of Paris there were once again those piteous cries of '*Nous sommes trahis*', and this time few Parisians doubted that they were nearly at the end of the line. The Buzenval battlefield presented a horrible spectacle; members of the American Ambulance told Washburne, 'the whole country was literally covered with the dead and wounded, and five hundred ambulances were not half sufficient to bring them away'.

For a total of only 700 Prussian casualties, the French had lost over 4,000 in dead and wounded, of which 1,500 were from the National Guard. The Government had at least succeeded in its aim of 'bleeding' the National Guard.

After Buzenval Trochu told his Government that militarily all was now lost, and that his own presence was 'no longer useful' – in so far as it had ever been. Meanwhile, in the Provinces, the Army of the Loire under Gambetta's general, Chanzy, had been decisively crushed at Le Mans. After some argument, an unlamented Trochu was replaced as military commander by General Vinoy, a tough old regular, but he retained the nominal office of President; while to Jules Favre was entrusted the invidious task of negotiating an armistice.

Now Belleville, overflowing with rage at the futile slaughter of its National Guards and in realisation of the imminence of surrender, erupted.

Shortly before one o'clock on the morning of 22 January, a band of armed men appeared at the gates of the Mazas prison, demanding the release of Flourens and the others imprisoned after 31 October. With drums beating, the insurgents then marched to the Mairie of the 20th Arrondissement, where they pillaged all the food and wine stored there, and set up a headquarters. Prudently, Flourens evaporated in the course of the night, but the following afternoon his liberators (no doubt inflamed by the looted wine) headed – once more – for the Hôtel de Ville. This time, no member of the Government was in the building, and Vinoy's forces were ready and determined, with armed Breton *Mobiles* behind every window.

Despite a warning given by Gustave Chaudey, a deputy of Jules Ferry, some two to three hundred National Guards reached the Place from the Bastille, armed to the teeth. The extremists leading them included the fanatical Louise Michel, clad in a *képi* and a man's uniform, and two of the lunatic fringe – Sapia, who had led the 8 October demonstration, and Jules Allix of *doigt prussique* fame. A solitary shot – fired probably, but not certainly by the insurgents – ignited the explosion. There were panicky shouts of 'They're firing on us', and Sapia's men knelt to fire a carefully directed volley into the Hôtel de Ville. Immediately a devastating fusillade crackled out of every window of the great building. Sapia was knocked down, mortally wounded. For the first time during the Siege, Frenchmen were killing other Frenchmen. It was a terrible omen of what was to come.

'The desperate crowd stampedes,' wrote Jules Claretie, 'tries to get away in all directions. The firing continues all the time. The windows of the Hôtel de Ville open and the *Mobiles* reply. People fall around me. On my left, I see a young man sink down in the yellow mud that has been diluted by a penetrating light rain; and on my right, a spectator in a top hat, killed outright.'

Louise Michel, who was to win her nickname 'the Red Virgin' that day, was driven to a frenzy by the sight of the mob being shot down. Firing from the cover of an overturned omnibus, she admitted shooting to kill and flayed those of her fellows who merely peppered the walls of the Hôtel de Ville. For half an hour the exchange of fire went on, until the arrival of reinforcements sent by Vinoy. The National Guard dissipated, overturning more omnibuses to cover its retreat, and leaving five dead and eighteen wounded – women and children among them – in the empty Place.

The 22 January uprising had been no full-scale attempt at revolution; the numbers of the insurgents were fewer than on 31 October; none of the principal 'Red' leaders – Delescluze, Blanqui, Pyat or even Flourens – was involved; and up to that day the great majority of the National Guard was still opposed to violence. But the shooting changed everything, and Paris hardened into two irreconcilable camps.

After 22 January, 'civil war was a few yards away,' Jules Favre wrote in retrospect, 'famine, a few hours'. Peace assumed a new, desperate priority. The very next day Favre began armistice talks. On the 27th, after Paris had been allowed the 'honour' of firing the last shot, the guns fell silent. Listening from a balcony of the Quai d'Orsay, Favre collapsed sobbing in the arms of his fifteen-year-old daughter.

News of the armistice was received in Paris with a mixture of rage and stupor. Edwin Child resigned in disgust from the *Garde*, which had never permitted him to fire a shot in anger, exclaiming: 'What an end of 20 years uninterrupted prosperity, and what a lesson to a nation fond of flattery and calling itself the vanguard of civilisation . . . !' The Left-wing *Rappel* growled, 'It is not an armistice, it is a capitulation . . . Paris is trembling with anger.'

And so ended the most disastrous war in the long course of French history. Compared with what it would cost to redeem this defeat half a century later, total French losses were not excessive; some 150,000 killed and died of wounds, and a similar number wounded (the German totals were only 28,208 and 88,488 respectively). During the Siege itself, French military casualties totalled 28,450, while deaths from all causes were set at just 6,251.

But, in Paris, the real killing had yet to begin.

NEITHER WAR NOR PEACE

With the coming of the armistice, hunger now eclipsed every other human emotion. Stocks of food were lower than estimated, with probably only a week's supplies left, at subsistence levels. The Prussians hastened to send in army rations, but it was to Britain and America that Paris chiefly turned in her hour of need. The response was immediate. Royal Navy ships were loaded up with Army stores; the Lord Mayor's Relief Fund was inundated with donations; while some $2,000,000 worth of food – a lot in those days – was expedited from the United States.

By 4 February, the first British food supplies began to reach Paris, and thereafter the trickle became a flood. But once again, as during the Siege, there were grave inequalities in the distribution of victuals; so the poor often remained acutely, and resentfully, hungry. Towards the end of the month an English doctor who had been in Paris throughout the Siege wrote: 'though fresh meat is to be had, the price is out of the means of the poor, and work is but slowly beginning. . . . I have seen more scurvy since the capitulation than I did during the Siege.'

Sooner or later the foodstuffs pouring into Paris would restore the bodies of the besieged, but it could do little to repair the insidious damage wreaked upon the minds and souls of Parisians. Psychologically, they were in anything but a fit state to face the humiliation of an unprecedented defeat, or of the crushing peace terms that lay ahead. Paris was grievously afflicted with a neurosis loosely diagnosed as 'siege fever', which, like the workings of an invisible parasite, had gnawed away progressively during the past months and only now revealed the full extent of its inroads. Boredom, malnutrition, the anxiety and uncertainty of what tomorrow would bring, the unbalancing effects upon a habitually highly-strung population of cycles of excessive optimism followed by blackest disappointment – above all the soul-destroying sense of isolation – these were among the causes which had produced the canker.

The symptoms of 'siege fever' were far from illusory. Describing a series of terrible nightmares she had suffered, Juliette Lambert recorded: 'For six days it seems as if all the centipedes in the world had traversed my brain and then attached themselves to it, and had to be torn off one by one, each time opening the seams of my mind.' Nerve tissue badly scarred by the Siege now had to cope with the deadly vacuum created by the capitulation. Paris had become a city of men shuffling aimlessly about, staring without purpose into shop-windows, like Britons on holiday; regular troops and *Mobiles* waiting to be sent back to their homes; National Guards with no employment; *petits bourgeois* with no trade. And in this vacuum, not far below the surface, a dangerous ferment was building up.

To escape from this oppressive atmosphere, all those who could began to leave Paris. The exodus was comprised principally from members of the middle-classes; which – it is worth noting – meant a substantial reduction in the strength of the bourgeois battalions of the National Guard on which the Government had relied to help keep order in Paris during the past months.

It would have required men profoundly versed in psychology to cope with the maladies of Paris; alas, the new leaders of France were to prove themselves as deficient in this respect as their predecessors had been in the conduct of war. With Trochu and Ducrot now fading into oblivion, on 8 February France went to the polls to elect a new Government which was to assume the responsibility of negotiating the peace terms offered by Germany. When the votes were counted, they revealed a crushing defeat for the supporters of Louis-Napoleon on one side and the Left wing on the other. Out of 768 seats, the vast majority had been won by deputies with conservative, Catholic and rural sympathies, of whom over 400 were assorted monarchists. No more than 150 genuine Republicans had been returned; only about twenty belonging to the extreme Left, mostly Deputies from Paris.

News of the elections hit Republican Paris like a thunderbolt. With the deeds and sufferings of Gambetta's levies concealed from their view, the Parisians in their neurotic state naturally concluded that they themselves had borne the principal weight of the war. '*Paris, c'est la France!*' had declared Danton. Paris, the centre of the universe, had bled and starved while the 'brutal rustics' stood by; and now they were carrying off the laurels of the peace. To the Left, murmuring of an electoral swindle, the results represented a defeat only less terrible in kind than the capitulation, and henceforth the peace-seeking, conservative country squires would become paired with the Prussian conquerors. Just as they felt they had been defrauded by the bourgeoisie and the provincials after each revolution during the past century, so now the Parisian proletariat began to fear that the glorious September Republic itself was in imminent jeopardy.

Every fresh act of the new Assembly, sitting far away at Bordeaux, widened the chasm between the provinces and aggrieved Paris. First, there was the choice of the man to lead the new Government: Adolphe Thiers. Although already seventy-three, Thiers's white-haired, gnome-like figure had lost none of its ruthless vigour. He was a consummate politician with almost half a century of experience in the tortuousness of French government, and an equally profound knowledge of French history. His first mentor had been Talleyrand, and he had helped Louis-Philippe to the throne. He had opposed Louis-Napoleon, had refused to take office along with the Republicans of 4 September, and once claimed: 'By birth I belong to the people; my family were humble merchants in Marseilles. . . . By education I am a Bonapartist; I was born when Napoleon was at the summit of his glory. By tastes and habits and associations I am an aristocrat. I have no sympathy with the bourgeoisie or with any system under which they are to rule.'

On the other hand, by instinct he was considerably less sympathetic towards poverty, or any of its manifestations. In 1834 when revolt threatened in Paris, Thiers as Minister of the Interior provoked the Parisian leaders into action with underhand cunning, then had them harshly crushed. For the 'massacre in the Rue Transnonain', immortalised by Daumier, the Left would always hold Thiers responsible, and it knew that it could now expect little but hostility from the new Assembly. A supreme realist, Thiers was also dedicated to concluding 'peace at almost any price' with Germany.

After some hard haggling, during which Bismarck had threatened to resume hostilities, a peace treaty was signed on 26 February. France was to lose all Alsace, and most of Lorraine, two of her fairest and most valuable provinces; including the bastion cities of Metz and Strasbourg. Thiers had managed to save Belfort – in return for subjecting Paris to the shame of a triumphal march by the conqueror. Initially demanding payment of an unprecedented war indemnity of six milliard francs, under British pressure the Germans had accepted five milliards – still an astronomical sum. (£200 million, or $1,000 million). 'The peace terms seem to me so ponderous, so crushing, so mortal for France,' groaned Goncourt, 'that I am terrified the war will only break out again, before we are ready for it.'

The Bordeaux Assembly ratified the Peace Treaty by 546 votes to 107, with twenty-three abstentions. Paris fumed in impotent rage and disgust. Gambetta and the deputies from Alsace-Lorraine resigned in a body; as did six of the extreme Left in Paris, including Rochefort and Pyat. They were followed by Victor Hugo, having been insulted by a rural *vicomte* who accused the old literary titan of not speaking French; yet another outrage to raw Parisian feelings.

There seemed indeed no end to the extent to which the Assembly could rub salt in the wounds of Paris. Next it announced that General d'Aurelle de Paladines was to take over as commander of the Paris National Guard; an unhappy choice, as d'Aurelle was a reactionary by repute, a former Bonapartist and violently anti-Parisian. He was also regarded in Paris, unfairly, as the man who had *failed* to come to her aid at the time of the Great Sortie. But it was clear that by this appointment Thiers intended to draw the teeth of the National Guard. Then, in a deplorable *ex post facto* ruling, Blanqui, Flourens and two other agitators were sentenced to death, *par contumace*, for their parts in the 31 October uprising.

But no act of the new Assembly caused more justifiable, and widespread, resentment than the Law of Maturities. This ordained that all debts, on which a moratorium had been declared during the war, were to be paid within forty-eight hours; while a similar law decreed that landlords could now also demand payment of all accumulated rents. The two bills were as cruel as they were stupid, and they dealt a staggering blow to hundreds of thousands of Parisians. With industry and commerce at a standstill for four months, and still virtually paralysed, only the wealthy minority had the funds with which to pay.

At the same time, as yet another measure designed to diminish the National Guard's potential, the Assembly voted to end the pay of 1.50 francs a day, which for so many had provided a form of dole during the Siege. Thus with these three unenlightened strokes a vast cross-section of Parisian society – the *petite bourgeoisie* of clerks and shopkeepers, artisans, and minor officials, few of whom owned their own dwellings – now found themselves thrust into the same camp as the underprivileged proletariat, whom they had hitherto despised and distrusted.

The last act at Bordeaux of this 'Assembly of country bumpkins', as Gaston Crémieux described it, was to adjourn itself on 10 March and decide (by 427 votes to 154) to reconvene in Versailles on the 20th. Mindful of the humiliation Trochu and Favre had been subjected to on 31 October, and of the shootings of 22 January, the Assembly certainly had reason to consider that somewhere outside of inflamed, disordered, atheistic 'Red' Paris would be more conducive to good government. The possible motives behind this latest slight were also apparent to the Parisians, but the choice of Versailles was taken as a sign not only of distrust, but – more dangerously – of weakness.

While the Bordeaux Assembly, in its heavy-handed insensitivity, was heaping injury upon injury on to wounded Paris, the city itself had been subjected to the worst humiliation that any proud capital can know – the ransom for Belfort, a Prussian triumphal entry and two-day 'possession' of the city. At 8 a.m. on 1 March 1871, a young lieutenant and six troopers of the 14th Prussian Hussars rode up to the Étoile, jumped their horses over the chains and other obstructions placed around the Arc de Triomphe by the Parisians, and continued unheedingly through the sacred edifice. Behind them followed thirty-thousand picked veterans of the war, passing in review before the newly-crowned Kaiser of Germany himself.

Two days later, sated with the meretricious joys of trampling on a crushed enemy, the triumphal troops withdrew, and Bismarck and his entourage departed for the Fatherland. At once Parisians set to scrubbing the streets the enemy feet had trodden with Condy's fluid, and 'purifying' the tainted *pavé* by the fire of many bonfires. But an atrocious stain had been left behind which nothing, save blood, would quite erase.

— 12 —

'RED' COUP AT MONTMARTRE

A casual visitor re-exploring Paris towards the end of February might well have been surprised at how swiftly the threads of life, broken by the Siege, were being picked up again; that is, if he kept to the relit *grands boulevards*. After the harsh winter, spring was just around the corner, and health was returning rapidly. Business was reviving, and traffic reappearing on the streets. People *seemed* more cheerful, and altogether there was an appearance of back-to-normal.

But it was thoroughly deceptive. Goncourt, though overjoyed to discover that his taste for literature was returning, found himself brooding over some indefinable malaise: 'something sombre and unquiet . . . upon the physiognomy of Paris. . . . Impossible to describe the ambient sadness which surrounds you; Paris is under the most terrible of apprehensions, apprehension of the unknown.' Observers outside the city walls found the 'unknown' a little easier to predict. Men with as different viewpoints as Lord Lyons, the British Ambassador, and the Prussian Crown Prince foresaw that an armed clash between the 'moderates' and the 'Reds' was now inevitable. 'How sad is the fate of this unhappy people,' added Prince Frederick with a sigh of genuine compassion.

'When you know Paris,' Trochu's aide wrote during the Siege, 'she is not a town, she is an animated being, a natural person, who has her moments of fury, madness, stupidity, enthusiasm.' She was about to embark upon one of her moments of fury, and her real mood might have been revealed by a savagely nasty incident occurring on the Place de la Bastille.

On 24 February, proletarian units of the National Guard had begun demonstrating there against suspected Government intents to disband them, coupled with protests against the German triumphal entry. It also happened to be the anniversary of the creation of the Second Republic in 1848, and the following day the demonstration had turned into a veritable Left-wing pilgrimage. The plinth of the July Column was heaped high with wreaths and oriflammes, and on the 26th the National Guard – its colours draped in black – participated in a mass march past lasting from morning till dusk. An estimated 300,000 Parisians took part, their tempers fired by much bombastic oratory.

Little was needed to create an incident. Abruptly the speeches were interrupted by shouts of 'A spy! A spy! Arrest him!' and a man was dragged forth, beaten and kicked. His name appears to have been Vincenzoni; his offence remains vague, but allegedly he was a Government spy noting down the numbers of *Garde* units involved in the demonstrations. Whatever the truth, the mob was lusting for blood, and the wretched man was dragged to the bank of the Seine, accompanied by yells of 'Beat him! Knock him on the head! Drown him!' Bound hand and foot, he was drowned amidst scenes of utmost brutality – under the eyes of several thousand unprotesting Parisian men and women.

That same day, insurgents forced their way into the Ste-Pélagie prison to release, among others, a prisoner detained for his part in the January disturbances; one Lieutenant Paul-Antoine Brunel, who was to play a key role in subsequent events. Brunel, a determined disciple of *résistance à outrance* during the Siege, had been arrested by Vinoy shortly before the capitulation, on charges of having ordered his men of the 107th Battalion of the National Guard to seize the magazines and telegraphs, and to forestall any attempt of the Government of National Defence to leave Paris by balloon.

Following the capitulation, the 'Red' battalions of the National Guard had gradually become grouped together under an executive organ calling itself the Comité Centrale de la Garde Nationale. By the beginning of March after additional units, disaffected by the Assembly's unpopular measures, had drifted into its orbit, and after many 'bourgeois' battalions had been disbanded owing to the mass exodus from Paris of their members, the Comité Central wielded huge potential powers. It, not d'Aurelle, the newly-appointed chief, effectively commanded the *Garde*, and when d'Aurelle on his arrival in Paris summoned a meeting of battalion commanders, only some thirty out of 260 turned up.

Now, on the same day as the lynching of Vincenzoni and the release of Brunel, aroused National Guards boldly descended on artillery parks in various parts of the city which the Germans were shortly to occupy during their triumphal visitation. Here they removed some two hundred cannon. Most of the guns bore National Guard numbers, and had been 'bought' by public subscription during the Siege. The *Garde* felt that these guns were 'their' property, and seemed genuinely concerned simply to prevent the shame of their falling into German hands. Chanting the *Marseillaise*, with prodigious physical efforts they hauled the cannon up to the 'Red' stronghold of Montmartre; strangely enough, without any clash with the regular army.

Thus, with startling suddenness, had the balance of power in Paris – and, indeed, France herself – changed. Under the Peace Treaty, the regular army had been reduced to only one division, so that the Paris National Guard – backed by its two hundred cannon – was now by far the most powerful armed force in France. All at once the Government became aware of the potential strength of the 'dissident' *Garde* – this Frankenstein being it had created during the Siege.

To Thiers, with his intimate recollections of past revolutions, the threat was far too grave to leave unchallenged. The regular army was ordered to recover the purloined guns; although, among the observing Prussians, General von Blumenthal doubted whether Vinoy, commanding the Paris garrison, could master the situation 'even with 40,000 men'. He was not far wrong. A feeble gesture made by Vinoy's men on 8 March was deflected by the *Fédérés* (as the 'Red' *Gardes* now called themselves), in whom a new toughness had become apparent. This display of weakness was followed up by the insolent burning-down of an Army barracks. Thiers then realised that a full-scale military effort would have to be made to cow the National Guard into handing over the guns. On 18 March, all the regulars at Vinoy's disposal – some 12,000 to 15,000, plus 3,000 gendarmes and police, went into action.

The main body of troops sent to recover the Montmartre guns consisted of two brigades; one of them commanded by a General Lecomte, the troops of which were largely young and inexperienced. There was little enthusiasm as the regulars reached their objectives under a glacial rain, before dawn that Saturday morning. Yet, like so many of the disastrous battles during the Siege, the operation began auspiciously enough. Although today's Montmartre would not yet have gone to bed, the regulars caught the village fast asleep. The guard-post in the Rue des Rosiers was captured, and locked up in the cellars of a restaurant close to where Gambetta had climbed aboard the *Armand Barbès*. By 4 a.m. it was all over, almost without blood-shed, and the vital guns were back in Government hands.

But, by a piece of almost unbelievable incompetence, typical of that professional ineptitude which had lost France the war, Lecomte's men now discovered that they had come without the teams of horses needed to tow away the guns. It was Cham-pigny, Le Bourget, and Buzenval all over again. Meanwhile, Louise Michel – the *vierge rouge* – escaping from her captors, ran down the hill to arouse the sleeping 'Reds' of Montmartre. Everywhere immense, hostile crowds composed of *Gardes* and the inevitable mixture of Parisian *canaille* materialised from thin air. Closer and closer they surged up to the regulars, whose officers were either too inexperienced or too dispirited to keep the mob at a distance. 'I have never been more embarrassed in my life,' said one captain. 'My orders were to disperse any assemblages, and the streets were nothing but one vast as-semblage in which my company was positively drowned.'

By 7.45 a.m. Lecomte's troops were all but submerged by the mob, pouring every kind of seditious argument into their young ears. Suddenly, some were seen to reverse their rifles, raising the butts in the air, accompanied by cries of 'Down with Vinoy! Down with Thiers!' The fury of the mob – goaded on by the tempestuous *vierge rouge* – now turned on General Lecomte, who had refused to allow a wounded *Fédéré* to be removed to hospital. His men having defected, Lecomte was hauled off his horse, insulted and beaten.

On the orders of the newly formed 'Vigilance Committee' of the 18th Arrondissement, consisting of Left-wing extremists like Clemenceau's Deputy Mayor, a bearded fanatic called Théophile Ferré, and against Clemenceau's intentions, Lecomte was dragged off to a National Guard post in the Rue des Rosiers. The procession, already composed of National Guards and some of Lecomte's own soldiers, collected some of the worst riff-raff of the Montmartre slums; including prostitutes and an appalling group of harpies who had been engaged in stripping an Army horse killed in the early scuffles. Figures horribly reminiscent of the *tricoteuses* of the Terror, they howled for the blood of the captive.

Shortly after Lecomte's arrival in this pleasantly named, peaceful suburban street, a new captive was brought in; a tall white-bearded old man wearing a frock-coat and silk hat. It was General Clément Thomas, the recently retired ex-Commander of the National Guard. They had seized Thomas on the Place Pigalle whither, it appears, he had foolishly been drawn by curiosity. Long hated for his part in crushing the 1848 Revolution, Thomas was now regarded by those into whose hands he had fallen as chiefly responsible for the massacre of the National Guard at Buzenval. His presence was in effect a sentence of death for both generals. Beyond all control, the mob burst into the house, demanding their immediate lynching.

A *Fédéré* captain rushed off to the Mairie to warn Clemenceau that the generals were in imminent danger. In his absence, however, General Thomas was taken out into the garden of No. 6 Rue des Rosiers. No proper execution squad was formed, and after a first ragged volley of shots the old general still stood there. Shot after shot was fired until he finally fell, with a bullet through the eye, insulting his executioners to the last breath. Lecomte was then dispatched too.

Some hideous scenes now ensued. The men continued to discharge their rifles into the dead bodies, while maenads from the mob squatted and urinated upon them. At this point, Mayor Clemenceau arrived – too late – shouting distractedly '*Pas de sang, mes amis, pas de sang*'. 'The Mob which filled the court-yard' said Clemenceau, 'burst into the street in the grip of some kind of frenzy. Amongst them were chasseurs, soldiers of the line, National Guards, women and children. All were shrieking like wild beasts without realising what they were doing. I observed then that pathological phenomenon which might be called blood lust. A breath of madness seemed to have passed over this mob'.

All that day Clemenceau, politically sympathetic towards the *Fédérés*, had been suffering from false optimism, first assuming that the guns would be delivered up without incident, and secondly that Lecomte would come to no harm. When he saw what had happened, he burst into tears, the last time, it was said, the tough doctor-politician was seen to weep in public until the victory of 1918. Momentarily even his own life seemed in jeopardy from the hysterical mob.

That evening, regular troops near the Invalides were astonished to see a carriage pass by, containing a gentleman in a grey overcoat. 'It was the Minister of War effecting his retreat in good order to Versailles.'

Since 5 a.m. that morning, the leading members of Thiers's Government had been waiting anxiously at the Quai d'Orsay as bad news succeeded bad. By the end of the morning, General Le Flô, the Minister of War, reckoned that no more than 6,000 National Guards could now be counted on as 'loyal'. The situation looked desperate; it was no longer merely a question of retaking the Montmartre guns, but of maintaining ascendancy in Paris itself. Thiers's sense of history now dictated a fateful decision: the Government would withdraw from Paris to Versailles, 'completely and immediately'. During the Revolution of 1848 it was what he had told Louis-Philippe to do –

'then return with Marshal Bugeaud and 50,000 men' – and he considered that, if his advice had been taken, the July Monarchy would still have been at the Tuileries. He would not permit the same mistake to happen twice.

Although there was some argument within the Government, it was settled by the appearance that afternoon of hostile National Guards on the Quai below. 'We're done for!' cried Le Flô. By a concealed staircase Thiers escaped into the Rue de l'Université, and, guarded by an escort hastily provided by Vinoy, he decamped to Versailles. The other Ministers followed shortly afterwards, and behind them marched the whole of Vinoy's regulars, jeered at by an annoyed Paris.

All the events of 18 March had taken the various 'Red' principals, as well as the Comité Central, thoroughly by surprise. None had anticipated the surprise Government move on Montmartre of that morning, nor the hideous retaliation it had engendered; but least of all had they foreseen that the Government, thwarted, would pull out. Just as on 31 October, no kind of contingency plan had been prepared.

While the Comité Central staggered, Paul-Antoine Brunel, a resourceful and effective leader who had been liberated on 26 February, seized the initiative himself as soon as he realised the Government was abandoning control. Gathering up some *Garde* units, he made for the Hôtel de Ville. After a brief exchange of fire, its defenders faded away through the subterranean passage which had served Trochu in such good stead on 31 October. Jules Ferry, now Prefect, made an undignified escape down a ladder, and Brunel found himself in possession of the building. Amidst tumultuous applause he unfurled a red flag from the belfry. For the first time since '93, revolutionaries were undisputed masters of Paris.

With the superior force now at their disposal, would they go on to seize control of all France?

— 13 —

THE COMMUNE TAKES OVER

'Paris could hardly be said to be "agitated"; the people promenading as usual on Sunday, and the National Guards marching along the middle of the streets. Indeed all had a completely holiday air.' Thus noted the Rev. Mr Gibson, an English Methodist clergyman who had spent ten years in Paris before the war, and was to remain throughout the Commune. It was the morning after Thiers had abandoned Paris to the 'Reds'.

There was unmistakably a festive atmosphere – at any rate in the proletarian districts – curiously reminiscent of the 4 September 'revolution' by which Louis-Napoleon had been overthrown. The only visible intrusion upon normal life was that 'the omnibus traffic was suspended'. Strolling round the Louvre, Edwin Child met 'many battalions of National Guards promenading, some for and some against the events of yesterday'.

In the bourgeois sections of Paris where he circulated, Goncourt, however, read 'on people's faces dazed indifference, sometimes melancholy irony, most often sheer consternation, with old gentlemen raising their hands in despair and whispering among themselves after looking cautiously all around'.

Inside the captured Hôtel de Ville, the scene was anything but calm. A widely diverse collection of 'revolutionaries' and dissidents of all hues was debating the situation that had been thrust upon them. All were astonished by it, most were overawed. Although later it became widely believed that 18 March had all been a plot carefully engineered by that sinister and shadowy group, the International, no one was more surprised than its leaders, including Karl Marx over in London. Everything that had happened that day bore the keynote of spontaneity. It was only on the initiative of junior commanders like Brunel that the abandoned Government offices had been occupied at all, and the Comité Central of the National Guard had organised nothing, planned nothing; with the result that it was now caught critically off balance. What course of action should be adopted? Who or what should fill the vacuum created by the departure of the Government?

Vigorously, and often chaotically, the argument raged. Brunel wanted to march on Versailles at once and arrest the Government, while Louise Michel was heard fiercely urging those who would listen to expedite the assassination of Thiers.

About all that emerged was the ascendancy of the Comité Central, which now assumed the burden of governing Paris, under the chairmanship of an ineffectual Marxist called Adolphe-Alphonse Assi, who had helped mount the big Le Creusot strikes in 1870.

Heatedly the killing of the two generals had been debated in those first sessions at the Hôtel de Ville. Neither the Comité Central nor any individual 'Red' leader bore responsibility for this spontaneous act of mob frenzy. Yet could they repudiate it? *Le Rappel* expressed profound grief, and even some of the most extreme Left-wingers were deeply shocked. But by and large the feeling was – recalling '93 – that such regrettable occurrences were unavoidable in revolutions. Thus, much to the propaganda advantage of Thiers, the Commune – by default – allowed itself to become associated with the deed.

Beyond the ranks of the revolutionaries, the news of the lynching of the two old generals had widely disgusted Frenchmen. Goncourt said he experienced a 'sensation of weariness at being French'. At Versailles, anger surged through the officers' messes of the regular Army, and with it went a grim determination to avenge Lecomte and Thomas. What little prospect there now existed of conciliation between the Government and the insurgents was made clear by Jules Favre when he declared, in tougher language than he had ever been known to use about the Prussians during the Siege: 'One does not negotiate with assassins.'

Yet, at this juncture, it was difficult to see how else Thiers was going to cope with the situation. The morale of the sadly depleted Army appeared to be very undependable indeed – as witness the defection of Lecomte's own troops. Each day brought renewed, and valid, fears of an overwhelming attack on Versailles by the insurgents, before ever Thiers had a chance to build up his own forces.

This was what Brunel had urged upon the Comité Central from the start, and Thiers was in fact saved only by the paralysis that confusion bred in the Hôtel de Ville – which ultimately would cause the ruin of all 'Red' dreams. In the dazed revolutionary councils there was no sense of urgency, no suggestion that a rebellion had been launched which any legitimate government would be bound eventually to suppress with force.

Most of the discussions turned on the essentially parochial political issue of Parisian autonomy, on the election of a municipal council, and on the repealing of the inequitable laws on debts and rents. The first military action of the Comité was mistakenly to place an unknown figure called Lullier – an alcoholic ex-naval officer discharged for bad conduct – in command of the National Guard, instead of the more obvious choice of Brunel. Apart from taking some quite unnecessary defensive precautions inside the Hôtel de Ville, Lullier did nothing.

For the rest, in those first days the Comité Central carried out none of the actions normally associated with revolutionary rule. Lord Lyons was agreeably surprised. To the Foreign Secretary he wrote on 21 March that its various proclamations in the *Journal Officiel* 'seem to me to be in form much more calm, dignified and sensible than the proclamations of the Government of National Defence used to be. . . . It is to be hoped that the Assembly will not make matters worse by violent and ill-considered resolutions.' All continued to be peaceful in Paris – which gave rise widely to belief in the possibility of conciliation.

With the withdrawal of the Government, the last vestiges of legal authority left in Paris were embodied in the Mayors of the Twenty Arrondissements. As early as the 19th, Thiers had instructed them to mediate with the insurgents; although his motives were rather to stall for time, which he so badly needed, than to attempt any genuine negotiation. The Mayors themselves were as mixed, politically, as the various districts they represented. They ranged from Tirard, the conservative Mayor of the second, the *arrondissement* of the banks and businesses, who was essentially Thiers's man, to Mottu of the ninth and Ranvier of the twentieth, who were supporters of Delescluze.

Most, however, were left of centre; while even the Right-wingers wanted Paris to gain some degree of municipal autonomy. All were anxious to avert any possibility of the situation heading towards civil war.

The most important of the Mayors was the radical Clemenceau, who was also a Deputy. Under his lead, contact was made between the Mayors and representatives of the Comité Central. To the insurgents, Clemenceau pointed out the illegality of their position; 'Paris has no right to revolt against France and must recognise absolutely the authority of the Assembly. The Comité has only one means of getting out of this impasse: give way to the Deputies and Mayors who are resolved to obtain from the Assembly the concessions demanded by Paris.'

For the Comité Central, Eugène Varlin responded by giving a surprisingly moderate list of demands: 'an elected Municipal Council . . . genuine municipal liberties, the suppression of the Prefecture of Police, the right of the National Guard to appoint its leaders and to recognise itself; the proclamation of the Republic as the legitimate Government, the postponement, pure and simple, of payment of rent arrears, a fair law on maturities . . .'

Until 4 a.m. on the 20th the talks dragged on. At last an agreement was reached whereby the Mayors would strive to get the terms of the Comité accepted by the Assembly; the Comité would hand the Hôtel de Ville over to the Mayors. But the next day the Comité Central came under heavy fire from more ardent revolutionaries for having been too weak and compliant in their dealings with the Mayors.

On the 21st the Comité informed Clemenceau that it was repudiating the agreement. This was a bitter blow for Clemenceau. From now on the Mayors were largely discredited by both parties, suspected by Versailles as being too extremist, and by the insurgents as being too moderate. The next day mediation was made still more difficult by a Thiers proclamation which, in uncompromising language, condemned the insurgents as 'senseless criminals'.

After the first paralysing shock had passed, a mild reaction had begun to build up in Paris. A motley of anti-revolutionary and 'moderate' elements, retired colonels, respectable shopkeepers, elderly brokers and remittance-men, as well as the remnants of the bourgeois National Guard had gravitated around Tirard's Mairie in the focal Second Arrondissement. Encouraged by emissaries of Thiers, they formed themselves into a body called the 'Friends of Order' and marched to demonstrate on 22 March, outside National Guard headquarters in the Place Vendôme.

They deliberately came unarmed – except for a few swordsticks and pistols secreted about the persons of some of the more nervous – and bore banners inscribed '*Pour la Paix*'. As they turned into the Rue de la Paix, they collided with the Fédérés under Bergeret, drawn up across the entrance to the Place Vendôme. Insults were exchanged and tempers rose, while all the time pressure from the rear was thrusting the leading 'Friends of Order' closer and closer on to the line of the *Garde*.

One knows how it happens; but one never knows which side fires first.

A lady trying on clothes in the *couturier* Worth watched the scene from the windows above: 'This mass of humanity walked down the Rue de la Paix, filling the whole breadth of it. One can't imagine the horror we felt when we heard the roar of a cannon, and looking down saw the street filled with smoke, and frightened screams and terrified groans reached our ears.'

Gaston Rafinesque, a young Parisian medical student marching with the 'Friends of Order', claimed that after the first volley, fired by the National Guard, 'the shooters started to march continuing to fire, which was why some of them were wounded by their comrades who were left behind . . .' When the firing died down, Rafinesque and another medical student helped pick up the dead and wounded; the first corpse they collected was that of an elderly gentleman wearing the Légion d'Honneur. The 'Massacre in the Rue de la Paix', as it became known, resulted in a dozen dead among the 'Friends of Order' and many more wounded, while Bergeret's men lost one killed and two or three wounded; it also brought the rift between Paris and Versailles beyond conciliation.

The Comité Central had meanwhile invested the military command of the National Guard in Brunel, Eudes and Duval – all raised to the rank of 'general' – in place of the bibulous Lullier who had (already) been arrested for incompetence. At Versailles, the talk was now all of 'suppression'. On the 25th, Thiers told Mayor Tirard: 'I hope that before two to three weeks we shall have a force sufficient to liberate Paris.' But when Tirard had asked for two regiments of gendarmes, he had been told, 'I have not got four men and a child to give you.'

In total defiance of the Assembly, and throwing to the winds earlier undertakings to the Mayors, the Comité Central now decided to hold municipal elections forthwith. On 26 March, Paris went to the polls. The results showed an indisputable advance in favour of the revolutionaries, compared with the 'plebiscite' held the previous November; it was proof of just how seriously Thiers and the New Assembly had alienated Paris.

Paris's new Municipal Council was controlled by 'Reds' in a proportion of four to one, and they promptly assumed the title of 'Commune de Paris', with all the awe-inspiring associations that conveyed. On Tuesday, 28 March, amid immaculate spring sunshine, it officially took residence at the Hôtel de Ville.

Superbly stage-managed by Brunel, for sheer spectacle it was a day of brilliance such as the city had not seen – paradoxically enough – since the braver days of the despised Louis-Napoleon. All Paris seemed to be there. In front of the Hôtel de Ville had been erected a platform decked in scarlet cloth on which stood the members of the newly elected Commune, also wearing red scarves, taking the salute as the massed units of the National Guard marched past. Never had this semi-trained militia, which had given so poor an account of itself during the Siege, marched with such a spring in its step. At 4 p.m. salvoes of cannon-fire pealed out from the captured guns. Assi, who stood near a bust of the Republic that wore a beribboned Phrygian cap, attempted to make a speech, but his words were drowned out by repeated roars of '*Vive la Commune!*' Abandoning his text, he shouted at the top of his voice: 'In the name of the people, the Commune is proclaimed!' and the crowd went mad.

'What a day!' exclaimed Jules Vallès, the novelist: 'O great Paris!'

There was little enough to cause anyone to reflect in this carefree moment that this day's events had brought France beyond the brink of civil war.

— 14 —

A FLAG IN THE WIND

'Now that our Commune is elected,' wrote an ex-corporal of the National Guard on 28 March, 'we shall await with impatience the acts by which it will make itself known to us. May God wish that this energetic medium will prove beneficial, and will procure us genuinely honest and durable institutions.'

Just what was the Commune going to do? First of all, what *was* the Commune – this mystical word 'murmured under the Second Empire, shouted under the Government of National Defence'? Even those who were to die unhesitatingly beneath its red standards could hardly give a coherent definition; and today one's fingers clutch awkwardly at vague slogans, conflicting ideologies and nebulous abstractions, additionally blurred by the flood of partisan propaganda over the years, of Marxist distortions and bourgeois vilification.

It is easier to define what the Commune was *not*. As of March 1871, it had nothing to do with Communism – despite the similarity in names. At that time Karl Marx sat in London directing a copious correspondence to the various branches of the seven-year-old International spread across the world. He had little regard for the French branch, whose leaders in 1868 he wrote off as 'ragamuffins'. His studies of 1848 made Marx most apprehensive of inadequately prepared popular revolts that went off at half-cock. Right up to 18 March, he had been strongly opposed to any uprising in Paris, and as Engels himself later admitted: 'The International did not raise a finger to initiate the Commune.'

At first taken unawares by its success, Marx suddenly, intuitively saw a vast potential significance in the new Paris revolution, and, with all the nimbleness of an incomparable opportunist, leapt aboard the bandwagon. In fact, it was the Commune that was to make Marx, and not the other way round.

In Paris, although the Rev. Mr Gibson in common with many of the bourgeoisie was convinced that 'most of the members of the Comité Central are members of the *International* Secret Society', these were actually a small minority, and even at their peak of influence there were never more than a score of Internationalists out of ninety on the council of the Commune. One leading Communard, Benoît Malon, even shocked Laura Marx by confessing he had never heard of *Das Kapital* and knew of her father only as 'a German professor'.

As compared with the revolutionaries of '48, however, the founders of the Commune were distinctly more proletarian. Even so, only twenty-one could be rated genuine workers (and none came from 'heavy industry'), while another thirty were journalists, writers, painters and assorted intellectuals; and thirteen were clerks and small tradesmen of the *petite bourgeoisie*; moreover, not one of the demands put forward at its inception in any way smacked of true Socialism, let alone of Marxism.

Not 'Communist', then, the Commune de Paris in fact predated Marx to 1789, when its precursor had been improvised simply to assume responsibility for administering Paris, following the fall of the Bastille. With the extremists taking over, in 1792 it was transformed into the 'Revolutionary Commune' which forced the Assembly to dethrone Louis XVI. By default, it then found itself for a time the real Government of France. Led by the violent Danton, on the one hand it firmly established the first French Republic, while on the other it successfully chased the foreign Royalist invaders from French soil; it was the combination of these two magical deeds that specifically first induced the 'Reds' during the Siege of Paris to reach back in history for the all-powerful amulet, *la Commune*.

As it came to power in 1871, the Commune was thus little more than a slogan with no platform, constantly glancing over its shoulder to 1793: 'The title was too imprecise to proclaim a programme, but, waving in the wind like a flag, it united the traditionalist souvenirs of some with the dreams of others and thus rallied French revolutionaries . . .' In the name of the Commune, its very diverse supporters tended to see their own personal Utopia, or a means of settling a grudge against, or dissatisfaction with, the established order.

Of grudges and dissatisfaction there was no shortage, the biggest backlog stemming from the poor social conditions inherited from the Second Empire: the appalling slums into which the workers had been concentrated through Haussmann's grand design; the vastly inflated cost of living; the long hours of work under deplorable circumstances; child labour still involving several thousands of eight-year-olds in Paris alone; no security of employment, no sickness benefits, no pensions. Rossel, a regular soldier of middle-class extraction who later threw in his lot with the Commune, was moved by what he saw among the Parisians under his command to exclaim: 'These people have good reason for fighting; they fight that their children may be less puny, less scrofulous, and less full of failings than themselves.'

There were also many attracted to the Commune simply by its face value; by its demands of municipal independence for Paris. Ever since the removal of the Revolutionary Commune that had terrified France, executive power over the city had been placed in the hands of the Prefect of the Department of the Seine, so that in effect any small rural community possessed more real autonomy than this great industrialised capital.

The two biggest factions dominating the Commune from beginning to end were the Jacobins, headed by Delescluze, and the Blanquists. Followers of Proudhon, the Blanquists were Socialists of the old school – except in the eyes of Marx, who considered them entitled to the name 'only by revolutionary and proletarian instinct'. Without any precise economic platform, they were violently hostile to the Church (almost the one issue on which all Communards were agreed) and to the regular army. They were for the most part dedicated revolutionaries, and even Marx had grudgingly acknowledged their leader to be the greatest revolutionary of the century. Auguste Blanqui, nicknamed '*l'Enfermé*', because of twenty-eight years spent in different prisons – was by far the most popular, and almost a legendary, figure among the Red leaders. Now sixty-six, his drawn, elongated features, white-cropped hair and thin beard gave him the look of a Greco apostle. The arch-priest of *résistance à outrance* during the Siege, it was Blanqui whose influence had lain behind most of the uprisings and demonstrations against the Provisional Government.

Still more lacking in any coherent programme was the large body of revolutionaries loosely classified as Jacobins. They were wedded to abstract ideas of political liberty, and were thoroughly conservative in the sense that they constantly looked to their namesakes of '93 for guidance: 'Their memory is always with me,' admitted one of them. They mistrusted Marx's new-fangled philosophy, and many Jacobins would have nothing to do with the Internationalists on the Commune. Their leader was Delescluze, the man around whom the mob had rallied on 31 October; his deeply eroded, tragic face still commanded support as well as sympathy, but at sixty-one he was prematurely worn out.

Then there was Rochefort, but – his aristocratic sensibilities possibly recoiling from the spectacle of the 'great unwashed' in command at the Hôtel de Ville, and little interested in social reform – he had not stood for election to the Commune. (Nor had that other great rhetorician, whose rodomontades had also done so much to inflame the Parisians to revolutionary pitch, Victor Hugo.) Also at heart a Jacobin was Pyat, Delescluze's pet aversion, whose paper appeared revivified as *Le Vengeur*, as scurrilous as ever and destined to become the principal organ of the Commune.

Among the Internationalist faction, the most outstanding figure was thirty-one-year-old Eugène Varlin, a handsome and intelligent bookbinder, one of the most sympathetic of the Communard leaders, and perhaps their most competent administrator. To Marxists Theisz and the Hungarian, Leo Frankel, the Commune was to owe most of the social legislation that it was able to achieve during its short life. Another interesting supporter of the International was the twenty-year-old illegitimate daughter of a Tsarist ex-cavalry officer, Elizabeth Dimitrieff, an elusive figure somewhat reminiscent of one of Dostoevsky's self-willed heroines, who by her glamour and plurality of lovers injected a certain glamour into the Commune. A close friend of Marx, she and Louise Michel became the principal organisers of the women under the Commune.

The redoubtable *vierge rouge* belonged to the anarchist faction; she too was a bastard, the progeny of a French *châtelain* and his chambermaid. Now forty, before the age of twenty she had fallen under the spell of Hugo. During the Siege, she had become a familiar, somewhat masculine figure, stalking into churches to demand money for the National Guard ambulances, wearing a wide red belt and seldom without a rifle (with bayonet fixed) slung from her shoulder.

After the anarchists, followed a nebula of assorted individuals: intellectuals, Bohemians, disgruntled *petits bourgeois*, general layabouts, *declassés*, and unclassifiables. In marked contrast to the rabble-rousing Louise, there was Paschal Grousset, a twenty-six-year-old journalist later appointed as the Delegate for External Affairs, a dapper little Corsican so carefully groomed that Rochefort nicknamed him the 'ladies' hairdresser', but whose intelligence and education favourably impressed Minister Washburne in his subsequent dealings.

The writers included Jules Vallès, permanently embittered by a youth of miserable poverty, and the already alcoholic Verlaine who was given a humble post as chief of the Commune press office. Then there was the painter, Gustave Courbet, gross and heavily bearded, and also sodden with drink, which made him look far older than his fifty-two years.

Among a number of largely apolitical soldiers of fortune came Flourens, and there was also a group of Polish exiles, including Dombrowski and Wroblewski who had both escaped after the Polish insurrection of 1863 and were to prove two of the Commune's ablest military commanders, attracted by the desperate belief that a blow for liberty anywhere was a blow for subjugated Poland. Motivated by less elevated ideals were pure terrorists like Montmartre's Théophile Ferré and the Bohemian layabout, Raoul Rigault, two sombre figures that come into their own in the final stages of the Commune. Finally, there were the representatives of the Red Clubs, still as full of wild and perfervid ideas as ever.

Thus, from the day it assumed office, the danger was apparent that the Commune might be overloaded, indeed overwhelmed, by the sheer diversity of desires as represented by so polygenous a multitude of personalities, ideologies, and interests. And there was no obvious leader to guide the multitude. Had Blanqui been there, it might have been quite a different story. But he had been picked up by Thiers's police on 17 March, and once again *l'Enfermé* languished in gaol. This was Thiers's best move to date; his 'great hope', so Lord Lyons reported to London on 30 March, 'appears to be that the members of the Commune will quarrel among themselves . . .' He had not long to wait.

On the night of the proclamation of the Commune, 28 March, its newly elected members met for the first time inside the Hôtel de Ville. At once there was an atmosphere of the fetid confusion prevailing in the Red Clubs. National Guards lolled, drunk or asleep, in corridors rank with tobacco smoke. Personal squabbles erupted, and there was immediate disagreement as to who should take the chair. Eventually the choice fell, by way of compromise, upon seventy-five-year-old Charles Beslay, as the oldest present.

There were lengthy debates on the vital issue as to whether or not the Commune should now march against Versailles; but these were confused by such abstract considerations as had the Commune been elected as a revolutionary body? The most practical view expressed was that the Germans might intervene. Could they indeed just stand by while the protagonists of *guerre à outrance* crushed the Government with whom they had just concluded so favourable a peace treaty? Nothing was decided, and the first session of the Commune broke up in discord and dissatisfaction after midnight.

The following day the Commune met again. This time it

managed to agree the formation of ten Commissions to carry out its various affairs. Heading the list was the Executive Commission, consisting of Eudes, Tridon, Vaillant, Lefrançais, Pyat, Duval and Bergeret. Despite its name, it had no executive powers, while in the background there was always the Comité Central of the National Guard to interfere with its workings; in fact, where the actual power of the Commune resided was never quite clear. Next in importance came the Military Commission, including Eudes, Bergeret, Duval and Flourens (the more impressive Brunel having already been dropped). To the key posts in the *Sûreté Générale* went the sinister pair, Ferré and Rigault.

The delegates of the various Commissions assumed their functions with positively unrevolutionary diffidence. When old Beslay − himself a failed banker − nervously arrived to 'take over' the mighty Bank of France, he found himself confronted by the imposing Marquis de Ploeuc and four hundred clerks armed with sticks. De Ploeuc engagingly appealed to Beslay's patriotism, reminding him that 'the fortune of France' lay in his hands. Beslay was overawed, and persuaded the Commune that − rather than seize the Bank − its finances could be assured by means of temporary loans from Rothschilds. He accommodatingly allowed himself to be installed in a small office next to de Ploeuc, completely under the latter's wing, while the astute Marquis smuggled out a steady flow of funds to Versailles.

This 'folly' later caused both Marx and Lenin to gnash their teeth; had the Commune grabbed the two milliards-worth of assets in the vaults of the Bank, 'the whole of the French bourgeoisie would have brought pressure to bear on the Versailles Government in favour of peace and the Commune'.

From 29 March onwards a flood of decrees began to pour out from the Commune, representing in their miscellany the extraordinary confusion over priorities that prevailed in the Hôtel de Ville. Great satisfaction greeted the repeal of the detested Rent Act, thereby exempting tenants from payment of rent for the previous nine months. Conscription to the regular Army was declared abolished; on the other hand all able-bodied citizens were to enroll for service with the National Guard. About the only other military measure taken at this time was the reoccupation of the southern forts which the regulars had abandoned, while it was sought to forestall any Versailles attack on the city by the following order sent to the officer guarding the western sector of the *Ceinture* railway: 'Place an energetic man at this post night and day. This man should mount guard equipped with a sleeper. On the arrival of each train, he must derail the train if it does not stop.'

Thus, as March drew to a close, the revolutionary masters of Paris had lost by their indecision thirteen priceless days since Thiers abandoned the city to them – days which Thiers himself had not wasted.

— 15 —

CIVIL WAR

Once the alarums and revolutionary zeal of those first days had quietened down, the bourgeois and uncommitted elements of Paris were agreeably surprised at how little changed life seemed to be. There had been few actual incursions into civic liberties. Two very hostile Right-wing newspapers had been seized, otherwise the rest continued unmolested. Between 18 and 28 March, the new Police Chief, Raoul Rigault, had arrested over four hundred people, but most of these (like Clemenceau) had been released again. There was no suggestion that a new Terror had been imposed on Paris; anti-Communards did not yet go to sleep in constant fear of the early-morning knock on the door.

Despite the disappearance of most of the Parisian police, judges and much of the civil service, order was surprisingly well maintained. There was little crime, and the Rev. Mr Gibson considered he had 'never seen the streets so well swept since the Siege'. Theatres were reopened, and, as the sunny spring weather settled in, so too did the euphoria of the simple supporters of the Commune.

To the under-privileged, the oppressed, the frustrated of Paris, these last few days must have possessed an unimaginable magic, must have been golden with promise. There is something about these days that reminds one a little of the tragic optimism of the Hungarian freedom fighters during the brief period of revolutionary liberty in 1956 – or Dubcek's Czechs of 1968 – while the Soviet tank divisions were being marshalled outside.

Doctors in Paris were somewhat astonished to learn that the

field hospitals had been closed down: 'Strange to say, it was not imagined then that any more fighting would take place.' Anaesthetised by debate in which fears of a Prussian reaction predominated, the Commune had shelved any plans for marching on Versailles. Together with the failure to seize the Bank of France, this was reckoned later by Marx to have been the Commune's cardinal error: 'the defensive is the death of every armed rising; it is lost before it measures itself with its enemies'. It was an error that his future pupil, Lenin, born the previous year at Simbirsk, would not repeat.

Thus the insurgents had lost the initiative, and gradually Versailles was permitted to regain its badly-shaken confidence.

By the first days of April, Thiers, through scraping the barrel all over France, had managed to muster a mixed bag of sixty thousand troops. No plan to reconquer Paris had been formulated, but on 30 March two squadrons of cavalry under the dashing Marquis de Gallifet, hero of the last desperate charge at Sedan, made a probe towards Neuilly. It succeeded in dislodging a small Communard outpost, encouraged Thiers and provoked the Commune, which now decided to march on Versailles in five days' time.

But Thiers acted first. Backing up Gallifet's reconnaissance, a strong attack was launched at Courbevoie (across the Seine from Neuilly) on 2 April, Palm Sunday. In Paris, Washburne experienced 'a singular sight' of being able 'to watch from the upper windows of my residence the progress of a regular battle under the walls of Paris'. For some time it was difficult to tell who was winning. Goncourt began his diary that day, welcoming the cannonade: 'Thank God! Civil war has begun.' But as time went on he noted gloomily: 'the cannonade dies away. Is Versailles beaten? Alas, if Versailles suffers the least reverse, Versailles is lost!'

Then, 'At last a paper told me that the Bellevillites had been beaten.'

It had been a repeat of Buzenval. After an initial success when one regular battalion had broken with ominous cries of '*Vive la Commune!*' the rebel National Guard – still no better trained or disciplined than in January – had panicked and fled back across the vital bridge at Neuilly. Small though it was, the success gave a great boost to the shaky morale of Thiers's forces.

Casualties were low, but one unpleasant incident had occurred which was to have endless repercussions. A much-beloved Dr Pasquier, Vinoy's chief surgeon, was shot down under a flag of truce, the Communards claiming it to have been a justifiable error. Whatever the truth, the killing caused great indignation among the loyal troops, and Thiers – condemning it as an atrocity on a par with the murder of Thomas and Lecomte – made maximum capital out of it.

Tempers were up. Trembling with rage at the Versailles attack, the Commune proclaimed hysterically: 'The Royalist conspirators have ATTACKED Despite the moderation of our attitude, they have ATTACKED.'

The boulevards 'were terribly agitated,' reported Edwin Child, 'at every turning almost were to be met battalions marching, their drums and clarions creating a most awful discord. On arriving Rue Royale, met them all united together and marching, so they said, straight to Versailles, but doubt if they will ever get there.'

At the Hôtel de Ville, there was the usual disunity, but eventually the Commune was rashly stampeded into launching a precipitate action the next day, 3 April.

The Communard force which set out westwards under Bergeret, Flourens and Duval was more of a mob than an army, approximating closely to the *sortie torrentielle* for which its leaders had pleaded throughout the first Siege. In its haste, the National Guard had omitted to take along its most powerful card – the two hundred cannon, the original *casus belli*, still languishing up at Montmartre.

The commanders, however, were full of confidence. Bergeret, a former bookseller's clerk, who arrived at dawn at the assembly area in a phaeton, caparisoned in sashes and great knee-boots that reminded one somehow of a Dumas musketeer, declared in a first dispatch: 'Bergeret *himself* is at Neuilly.' Flourens, magnificent as ever in his Cretan uniform – blue pantaloons, immense scimitar, and Turkish belt crammed with pistols – telegraphed back to the Hôtel de Ville: 'We shall be the victors . . . there cannot ever be a doubt of that.'

It all reminded a Communard chronicler, Edmond Pelletier, tragically of 'a horde of turbulent picnickers, setting out gaily and uncertainly for the country, rather than an attacking column directing itself towards a formidable position'. As they sauntered across the Seine, shells from powerful Fort Mont-Valerien (which the Communards had foolishly neglected to occupy after 18 March) fell devastatingly in their midst.

The column split in two, the rear fragment scattering rearwards across the river. At the head of the column, Flourens characteristically persisted in pressing on towards Versailles, but was soon deserted by Bergeret and his force. Abandoned, he dossed down at an inn, where he was seized – without arms. A gendarmerie captain, apparently recognising him, cleft his head in two with one savage sabre blow.

Thrown upon a dung-cart, the corpse of the flamboyant adventurer was wheeled in triumph to Versailles (where, reportedly, elegant ladies submitted it to unmentionable indignities). Elsewhere, at least five captured Communards were also executed summarily by order of Gallifet, presumably as reprisals for the killing of Dr Pasquier. The next day Government troops captured Duval too, and on his way to Versailles he was intercepted by Vinoy himself. Addressing them as 'hideous scum', Vinoy ordered Duval and three others to be shot out of hand. The terrible escalation of atrocities that is the inevitable feature of civil war was now beginning.

After the Commune's first military disaster, the Rev. William Gibson found National Guardsmen wandering about in twos and threes, looking extremely dejected: 'fatigued and worn, covered with dust; so changed in their appearance from what they were when they marched out on Sunday evening'. At Père Lachaise cemetery, muffled drums beat and women sobbed as dead heroes of the Commune were buried in an imposing state funeral.

At the Hôtel de Ville, the Commune rulers had reacted to

the first military reverses in the true revolutionary spirit of '92. Assi and Lullier, suspected of treachery in their negligence at not occupying Mont-Valérien, were promptly flung into prison, followed shortly by the over-confident Bergeret. But this dismal failure was quite overshadowed by indignation and fury at the killing in cold blood of Duval and the other captured National Guardsmen. There was much talk about exacting 'an eye for an eye, a tooth for a tooth'. An obscure Communard called Urbain now introduced a measure that was to gain everlasting notoriety as the 'Law of Hostages'.

This decreed as follows: every person accused of complicity with Versailles would be imprisoned; juries to be instituted to try these parties within forty-eight hours; those convicted to be held as 'hostages of the people of Paris'; and the execution of any Commune prisoner-of-war to be followed immediately by the execution of three hostages, 'drawn by lot'. Who would be the hostages? A new chill of uneasiness settled over the anti-Communard elements of Paris; Goncourt predicted gloomily, 'If Versailles does not hurry up, we shall see the rage of defeat turn itself into massacres, shootings and other niceties by these tender friends of humanity . . .'

But Thiers was in no hurry. He felt he could not yet rely too much on his regulars. There were still disquieting *défaillances*, soldiers going over to the Commune. So he now settled down to 'regroup' his forces.

Meanwhile, Favre, the negotiator, was at Prussian Head-quarters obtaining permission to increase the French Army beyond the limits imposed by the Peace Treaty. Bismarck, at first cynically neutral towards the humorous spectacle of Frenchmen killing Frenchmen, was now nervous as to the impact the Commune might have upon his arch-enemies at home, the Social Democrats, and he was content to allow Thiers's army to inflate by stages to 170,000 men. In the provinces, risings in sympathy with the Commune had all fizzled out, or were about to be crushed, that in Marseilles ending in the slaughter of 150 rebels in the captured Prefecture.

For the second time within a matter of months, it looked as if the tragic city was going to be cut off and isolated from the rest of the world. Foreseeing what lay ahead, non-Communards began leaving the city by the thousand, while they still could, or else went into hiding to avoid conscription into the National Guard.

16

THE SECOND SIEGE

Inside the military command of the Commune, the death of Duval and Flourens, plus the imprisonment or dismissal of Brunel, Lullier, Eudes and Bergeret, had created a considerable vacuum. A new figure was now drawn into it: Gustave Paul Cluseret. Aged forty-seven, Cluseret was a true soldier of fortune like Flourens; less romantically appealing, but with an even more remarkable career as an adventurer, and a much wider military background.

Commissioned at St. Cyr, Cluseret had helped crush the 1848 risings. After being wounded in the Crimea, he was cashiered for 'irregularities' concerning army stores in Algeria, and then went off to America in pursuit of his fortunes. He enlisted as a volunteer on the side of the North during the Civil War, and – startlingly – was promoted Brigadier-General after a brief spell as ADC to McClellan; but incompetence caused him to be relegated to an insignificant post in Baltimore. Next he appeared as 'general-in-chief' of the Fenian cause in England, taking part in the 1867 attack on Chester Gaol. With England too hot for him, he returned to France where he was soon before the courts for seditious activities.

With a cheroot constantly clamped in the corner of his mouth – a habit picked up during the Civil War – Cluseret was both cynical and lazy, and managed to inspire universal mistrust. He reckoned the prospects of Paris in April no greater than had Trochu during the First Siege – and, as a one-time regular, he shared the latter's contempt for the National Guard – an opinion which he was disastrously incapable of keeping to himself. But at least he had had more practical experience than any other Communard.

After the catastrophe of 3 April (he said it reminded him of Bull Run), Cluseret ordered the Commune forces to take up a strictly defensive posture behind the forts and ramparts which had kept Moltke out for so many months. In the breathing-space granted by Thiers's regrouping, he settled down leisurely to reforming the National Guard. The hour was very late indeed, and the task Augean. Bad habits acquired during the First Siege had become deeply rooted. At least two of the battalions in action at Courbevoie had been 'completely drunk'. Discipline was non-existent. 'Never,' said Cluseret on his take-over, 'have I seen anything comparable to the anarchy of the National Guard. . . . It was perfect of its kind . . .'

With nothing resembling staff-work, a proper commissariat or communications service, it was little wonder that the artillery had been left behind on 3 April. Battalion commanders were constantly being sent hither and thither by conflicting orders emanating from their own headquarters in the Place Vendôme, from the Comité Central, or from the Military Commission of the Commune, as well as from local functionaries in each Arrondissement, none of which seemed to have any seniority over the others. 'There were almost everywhere independent chiefs, who did not accept or did not carry out orders . . .'

Following the example of the Tirailleurs (now rechristened the Vengeurs) de Flourens, a proliferation of private armies had sprung up. Each was costumed bizarrely and extravagantly according to the whim of its commander. Even Madame Eudes, a striking and not noticeably proletarian figure who liked to be known as *la générale Eudes*, often appeared either as a pistol-packing Amazon, or 'like the Empress, in *gants à huit boutons*'. Cluseret's first measure was to decree 'no lanyards, no more glitter, no more gold braid', and at the same time to abolish the rank of general. His next reform − to split the National Guard (as Trochu had attempted during the Siege) into 'active' and 'sedentary' battalions − made him even more unpopular.

Undoubtedly Cluseret's greatest contribution lay in his choice of subordinates: Rossel as his Chief of Staff, and the thirty-five-year-old Polish nobleman, Jaroslaw Dombrowski, as Commandant of Paris. These were to prove the Commune's two ablest officers, and it was greatly owing to Dombrowski's talents in the field and to Rossel's energy in carrying through Cluseret's reforms that the Commune forces began to show a striking improvement. On 9 April, two Montmartre battalions managed to inflict a sharp reverse on Versailles forces during a surprise night attack, and even Goncourt – no friend of the Communards – was asking himself: 'Why this stubborn resistance which the Prussians did not encounter?'

Thiers was keeping up the pressure at Neuilly, and throughout most of April fighting surged back and forth from street to street. From behind barricades built of ripped-up *pavé*, Dombrowski's men stood up to an attack consisting chiefly of devastating and persistent artillery fire that echoed across Paris. Now on the defensive, with their backs to their homes instead of being employed on ambitious offensive tactics, the Communards gave a good account of themselves. Each day resistance increased with familiarity.

Casualties were not light. A British ambulance worker was shocked to see the wretched condition of the wounded, still suffering from the after-effects of the First Siege, superimposed upon years of deprivation: 'What pains me most is not the wounds, but to see their poor shrivelled legs, really not larger than a strong man's thumb.'

The mortality rate among the wounded was discouragingly high: 'I am sorry to say that it is the old story, out of 40 cases operated on hardly one recovers. Drink, drink, drink; there is always the smell of drink . . .' The ill-equipped, disorganised hospitals, reeking of gangrene, found themselves forced to add carbolic acid to bottles of surgical alcohol, because it 'disappeared at one time so rapidly' down the throats of the orderlies.

Not only the combatants were suffering. The prosperous village of Neuilly, largely spared during the Prussian bombardment, was being progressively destroyed, with many of its inhabitants trapped in the ruins. By the end of April: 'Every single tree is cut in pieces, and the ground is covered with grape, canister, shot, and broken shells and flattened bullets. I entered what had been beautiful houses, with floors wobbling and held up only by a side, utterly wrecked. . . . In many houses we found the dead laid out, where they had been placed some days ago . . .'

As fresh guns and ammunition became available to Thiers, the bombardment spread to other suburbs in the west of Paris. One morning Goncourt, working in his garden at Auteuil was driven into the cellar by the 'whistling of several shells'. For nearly two hours the bombardment continued, and he emerged from his cellar to find that three immediately adjacent houses had been hit.

Ironically, it was the most staunchly anti-Communard parts of Paris that were bearing the brunt of Government gunfire. Occupants of Passy were convinced that the defenders ('a dirty, lewd, sordid, vicious, indisciplined rabble') had deliberately sited their guns so as 'to draw cannon-balls down' on this detested bourgeois quarter. Soon the shells from Mont-Valérien were reaching out still further into the centre of the city, as haphazardly as at any time during Moltke's bombardment. Washburne recorded shell splinters striking the US Legation near the Étoile 'within twenty feet of where I was writing'; while two days later he counted twenty-seven separate hits on the Arc de Triomphe itself.

After watching in horror as a shell carried off both legs of a seventy-year-old lady outside his church, Edwin Child declared angrily: 'At one time I was almost French in sentiment, but now I scorn them almost as much as I do the Germans.' Like many Parisians, by the end of April he was wishing 'the whole affair was finished one way or other. It is becoming absolutely sickening, during the siege at least people knew why they were suffering and for what end, but now it would be difficult to say which is the most preferable, the Commune or the Government. Both give such proofs of their incapacity . . .'

Thiers and MacMahon had now formed a tentative plan of

campaign. The Achilles' heel of the Communard defences seemed to lie at the Point du Jour, the extreme south-western tip of the city, close to where the Seine flows out towards Sèvres. It was here that his army would try to break in. But first they would have to capture Fort Issy, the imposing fortress controlling the approaches just across the river. Disengaging from Neuilly, under cover of a truce, MacMahon transferred fifty-three batteries against Fort Issy on 25 April. Two days later he succeeded in pushing a parallel to within 300 yards of Issy; by then it was 'no longer a fort, hardly even a fortified position; a litter of shell-lashed earth and rubble,' said Lissagaray.

By 30 April, the Communard commander – Mégy, a work-man who had killed a policeman the previous year – evacuated the fort, after vain pleas to Cluseret for reinforcements. Cluseret, having had only four weeks in office, was worn out by the intrigues and wrangling within the various organs of the Commune. Yet, on hearing the news from Issy, he summoned up a rare burst of energy, and marched out himself with two hundred men to see what could be retrieved of the situation. To his surprise, he found the fort just as Mégy had left it, unoccupied; with the exception of 'an urchin of sixteen or seventeen, weeping quietly upon a barrel of gunpowder,' whose intentions were to blow up the fort and himself when the enemy entered.

Cluseret unspiked the guns and re-garrisoned the fort. By a miracle he had saved Issy, but he could not save himself. On returning to Paris, he was met by a picket and placed under arrest.

'Incapacity' was the reason officially given for Cluseret's arrest, but Paris buzzed with rumours that he had been plotting to overthrow the Commune; that he had sold himself to Versailles. It was an indication of the new nervousness within the city. An obsession about treachery within was the successor to the 'spymania' of the First Siege, in a much more pungent form.

Cluseret was replaced by his Chief-of-Staff, Louis Rossel. Completely apolitical, Rossel was one of the more unusual adherents to the Commune, and his attachment testified to how the bitterness felt by so many loyal Frenchmen at the January surrender had led up to the March insurrection. At this distance in time, he, Varlin and Delescluze strike one as being – in their different ways – the Commune's three most sympathetic figures. But Rossel, at twenty-six, was also by far its most efficient soldier. Had he been in charge in March, subsequent history might well have been different; had he survived, it seems almost certain that he would have left a mark of genius somewhere.

Born of a Scottish mother, Rossel had been a regular in the Engineers. As a captain in Bazaine's army, in disgust he toyed with the idea of 'deposing' the Marshal; then escaped from capitulated Metz disguised as a peasant. He made his way to join Gambetta, who – recognising genius in this strange, fierce young man with a straggly black moustache and penetrating eyes – promoted him colonel.

Rossel was appalled by the armistice: 'We are wanting in patience; we conclude peace as rashly as we went to war.' The day after the insurrection in Paris, he wrote to the Minister of War, resigning his commission and announcing: 'I do not hesitate to join the side which has not concluded peace, and which does not include in its ranks generals guilty of capitula-tion . . .' Then he set forth to Paris, in the hopes that he could somehow 'snatch back victory' from the Prussians. Socialism, Blanqui, Marx meant nothing to him: 'I did not know who the insurgents were, but I knew against whom they were rebelling, and that was sufficient.'

With his engineer's eye and revealing an energy never seen in Cluseret, Rossel ordered the immediate construction of a ring of barricades behind the ramparts; a second line of defence in the event of MacMahon breaking through the perimeter. Inside the city, three last-ditch 'citadels' were to be erected at the Trocadéro, Montmartre, and the Panthéon on the Left Bank. The whole of the south side of Paris was now entrusted to another courageous and competent Pole, thirty-four-year-old Wroblewski. For the first time, Rossel attempted to concentrate the Commune's powerful artillery, some 1,100 pieces scattered uselessly about.

17

BY ORDER OF THE COMMUNE . . .

While on the one hand fighting for survival, the Commune persisted in its zealous aims of reforming the world. On 2 April, the Church was disestablished – one measure on which all factions were united. Gambling was banned, pawnshops suppressed, and efforts made to combat prostitution. Somehow time was found to issue an *ordonnance* about the Ham Market, specifying that Parisians should not relieve themselves 'elsewhere than in the public urinals'. Throughout April and into May, a mass of legislation poured out from the Hôtel de Ville: a mixture of incredibly irrelevant trivia and genuine attempts to right social injustices.

Fines on workers were abolished, and salaries of all Government officials limited to 6,000 francs a year, roughly equivalent to a workman's wage. On 16 April, an edict ordained the 'nationalisation' of workshops abandoned by their bourgeois owners (but it was never carried out). On the 28th, nightbaking – long a grievance among the bakery workers – was ended (Frankel, responsible for the bill, considered it the Commune's one big achievement; while the residents of Passy grumbled that it only meant 'all Paris is reduced to stale bread'). All the wives and children of men who died 'in defending the rights of Paris' were to be 'adopted' by the Commune; the wives – 'married or not', the Rev. Mr Gibson was shocked to discover – were to receive pensions of six hundred francs a year.

In cultural affairs, the Commune was busily preparing

legislation to laicise schools, while Courbet was charged with re-establishing the annual salon.

Going to the Hôtel de Ville to appeal for the release of the hostages arrested in April, Henri Dunant, the founder of the Red Cross, had a vivid insight into the chaos surrounding the legislature of the Commune: 'There was a mob of petitioners of every kind, National Guards, women with little children, crazy people and all kinds of hungry sufferers, all mingling in a motley crowd . . . or sprawling in the brocaded easy chairs, eating, smoking, snoring, or just sitting quietly, playing cards and swearing in low voices, cursing, scolding and drinking too. But how much real misery there was, and what heartache! . . .'

On 19 April the Commune issued what was probably its most imposing and important politicosocial proclamation. In immense placards posted throughout Paris it declared the aims for which it was fighting: 'the recognition and consolidation of the Republic . . . the absolute autonomy of the Commune extended to all the localities of France. . . . The absolute guarantee of individual liberty, of the freedom of conscience and the freedom of labour . . .'

Paris herself reserved the rights to make 'administrative and economic reforms demanded by her population . . . to universalise power and property according to the necessities of the moment, the wish of those interested, and the rules furnished by experience . . .'

Rising to a powerful, grandiloquent climax, the proclamation continued: 'The Communal Revolution, begun by the popular initiative of 18 March, inaugurates a new political era, experimental, positive, scientific. It is the end of the old governmental and clerical world, of militarism, of monopolism, of privileges to which the proletariat owes its servitude, the Nation its miseries and disasters.'

This was, in essence, the Commune's testament; certainly its closest approach to formulating any coherent programme. But nothing the Commune said or did faced up to the issue over which so many patriotic Parisians had originally sided with it –

the humiliation of the lost war. Nor, patently, had it ever had the military potential for any such action.

On 16 April, with the fighting at Neuilly at its peak, the Commune Assembly held by-elections to fill thirty-one vacancies created by the resignation of disillusioned moderates, by deaths and other forms of erosion. The new blood did little to improve matters. As the pressure from Versailles mounted, so did the bickering within, with Pyat, as ever the irresponsible polemicist, usually to be found somewhere near the eye of the storm. Each legislation threatened to split the Commune up into its diverse components. 'None of this would matter,' Marx warned Varlin by letter, 'if you had the time to recover the time already lost.' Clearly, it did not have the time.

'What gnawed the heart of the Commune,' declared Rochefort with reason, 'was distrust. The Hôtel de Ville distrusted the Ministry of War, the Ministry of War distrusted the Ministry of Marine, Vanves Fort distrusted Montrouge, which distrusted Issy. Raoul Rigault distrusted Colonel Rossel, and Félix Pyat distrusted me.' Delescluze was disgusted by it all, and in a fiery speech magnificent for one so sick and worn out he thundered to the Commune assembly: 'You complain that our decrees are not carried out. Well, citizens, are you not yourselves somewhat accessory to this fault? . . . When a decree appears in the *Journal Officiel* with 13 negative votes and only 18 in the affirmative, and does not meet with the respect that this assembly deserves, can you be astonished?'

'You should have replaced us sooner,' he went on.

Finally, after three days of stormy debate, on 1 May a 'Committee of Public Safety' – so redolent with associations of Robespierre and the Terror – was created to take over the Commune's executive functions. But the voting, 45 to 23, split the Commune henceforth into a Majority and a Minority faction: the one, controlled by the Jacobins, wanting to exercise dictatorship and terror – the methods of '93; the other (including Beslay, Courbet and Varlin) desiring to govern by reasonably democratic and moderate means, leaving 'the door at least half open to conciliation'.

Of all the leaders of the Commune, none was more responsible for its final, savage image than Raoul Rigault. A Bohemian frequenting the revolutionary haunts of the Left Bank in prewar days, Rigault was an instinctive Jacobin, who spent most of his leisure time plunged into books about the Terror. From his researches, he had concluded that Saint-Just was merely a feeble amateur in the art of terror, and he had set himself to studying modern police techniques. About him and his faithful lieutenant, Ferré, there was a touch of cold, twentieth-century professionalism, a suggestion of a Beria or an Eichmann, notably lacking in the rest of the Communards.

'I want sexual promiscuity. Concubinage is a social dogma,' declared Rigault, practising what he preached. Though he was only twenty-five, debauchery had probably aged him, as he was described by one potential victim as 'a man about thirty-five or forty years old, short, thick-set, with a full round face, a bushy black beard, a sensuous mouth, and a cynical smile. He wore tortoiseshell eye-glasses; but these could not hide the wicked expression of his cunning eyes.'

On the fall of the Empire, Rigault had promptly offered his services to the Prefecture 'to dig out secret agents of the Bonapartist police, arrest them and prosecute them . . .' He had attempted to make himself Prefect of Police on 31 October, and finally the coveted post was granted him on 20 March. But a month later protests against Rigault's arbitrary arrests had reached such a peak that both he and Ferré were sacked. On 27 April, however, he re-emerged vested in the immensely greater authority of Procureur of the newly-created Revolutionary Tribunal – yet another title with unpleasant connotations from '93, and under it Rigault wielded more real power than any other member of the Commune.

It was on 4 April that Rigault had initiated the deed by which his name will be longest remembered. He arrested the Archbishop of Paris, Monseigneur Darboy. This was later followed by the wholesale round-up of priests. Between a Jesuit and the atheistic Rigault, acting as interrogator, a famous interview took place:

Rigault: What is your profession?
Priest: Servant of God.
Rigault: Where does your master live?
Priest: Everywhere.
Rigault (*to a clerk*): Take this down: X, describing himself servant
of one called God, a vagrant.

Excuses of varying transparency were given for the arrests,
but it happened that they coincided closely with the passage of
the 'Hostages Bill', which received strong support from Rigault.
There was a motive deeper than mere hatred of the clergy; one
that would become grimly familiar a hundred years later.
Rigault was obsessed with the belief that, for the Commune to
survive, it had to have the imprisoned Blanqui to lead it.
'Without Blanqui, nothing could be done. With him, everything.' Thus Rigault despatched one of the arrested priests with
a letter to Thiers, proposing to swap the hostage Archbishop for
Blanqui. But Thiers, reacting more toughly than most modern-
day politicians, refused; to hand Blanqui to the Commune, was,
he calculated, 'to send it a force equal to an Army Corps'.

For all the energy and sense Rossel had tried to inject into the
conduct of the war, things did not go much better for him than
for Cluseret. The Committee of Public Safety proved to be one
more bureaucratic millstone around his neck. Then, on the
night of 3 May, there was a disaster at Moulin-Saquet when 800
National Guards were caught in their sleep by a surprise attack;
50 were slaughtered and a further 200 captured, for a cost of
only 36 Versailles casualties. But it was at Issy that the most
important fighting continued. In response to a Government call
to surrender, Rossel wrote back defiantly:

'My dear Comrade,
    The next time you send a summons so insolent as that
contained in your yesterday's letter I shall have the man who
brings it shot, according to the usages of war.
    Your devoted comrade,
    Rossel.'

The National Guards were fighting there better than they ever had, against bitter odds. One by one the fort's guns had been knocked out; there were no doctors, and provisions were running out. On 5 May, one of the fort's officers wrote in his diary: 'All our trenches, smashed in by artillery, have been evacuated. The Versailles parallel is within 60 metres of the counter-escarpment. They are advancing closer and closer . . . 7 May. We are now receiving up to ten shells a minute. The ramparts are completely uncovered. . . . With the exception of one or two, all the guns have been knocked out. The Versailles earthworks are now almost touching us. . . . We are on the point of being surrounded.' Disgracefully, Eudes, the nominal commander at Issy, had found an excuse to pull out, leaving his deputies to bear the brunt.

Rossel decided to launch a sudden offensive blow to relieve the doomed fort. But the troops defected. In a fury, he personally punished a number by cutting off their right sleeves, 'commencing with the officers. They were all sobbing . . .' His action was bitterly resented, and the next day several battalion commanders, who had pledged troops for the attack, defaulted. This was the last straw for Rossel, and on 8 May he sent in his resignation. For Fort Issy, having suffered over 500 dead and wounded, this also was the death-knell.

A session of the Commune was interrupted by Delescluze with the gravest news it had yet received: 'You argue,' he cried, 'while it has just been announced that the *tricolore* now floats over Fort Issy! Treachery threatens us at every hand. . . . Today the National Guard no longer wants to fight, and you discuss matters of procedure. We shall still save the country, though possibly now only behind barricades.' But, he begged, 'put away your mutual hatreds'. Deeply moved, the Commune applauded loud and long.

Two days later Rossel was warned by a friend that he was to be court-martialled. The insurgents' brightest, and last, military star now leaped into a carriage and disappeared, not to be seen again during the life of the Commune.

From Versailles, Thiers issued a proclamation to the Parisians warning them that the general attack on the city was about to begin: 'The moment has now come when, to shorten your sufferings, [the Versailles Army] must attack the fortifications themselves . . .'

18

FLORÉAL 79

News of the flight of Rossel struck Paris like a thunderclap. But doomed though it might be, the Commune was far from dead, and it now gave power to the one man who could rise above its petty factionalism, and inspire it in its last agonies: Delescluze. The sixty-one-year-old Jacobin who had led the attempted insurrection against Trochu on 31 October was himself slowly dying of consumption contracted through long years on Devil's Island. 'He no longer spoke, he hardly breathed,' said Rossel. But when he did speak, every Communard listened.

The son of a '92 revolutionary, by the time he was an adolescent Delescluze had already done his apprenticeship at the barricades. Unshaven, with dirty hands and nails, he dressed shabbily à la Marat with a coarse kerchief around his neck. His face was described by a contemporary as 'eroded into deep wrinkles and strange zigzags denoting what Balzac described as the defeats of private life'.

Yet there was something strangely noble about the dying Delescluze. He was as incorruptible as Robespierre, and every Communard knew that he would go on to the bitter end. The powers now accorded him were total. On the eve of disaster, something approaching control of the Commune was at last invested in one pair of hands; those of its most outstanding personality. But at the same time the ascendancy of Delescluze completely changed its character. For he was the king Jacobin, as backward-looking as any restored Bourbon. Promptly, the new Committee of Public Safety began to date its proclamations with the old calendar of the Great Revolution, starting on '15th

Floréal, year 79'. Jacobinism revived meant social reform taking second place to the heroic traditions of '93, which in turn spelled out – the Terror. Behind Delescluze stood the savage figures of Ferré, and the murderous hippie, Raoul Rigault.

With each fresh military setback, the actions of the Jacobins grew more desperate. The Grand Hotel was sacked; there were repeated threats to confiscate all private property; hostile newspapers were suppressed; mounting 'spymania' caused the arrest of many innocent Parisians (including Renoir, who narrowly escaped lynching while working at his easel). Only the collapse of the Commune was to save the destruction of the Chapelle Expiatoire, erected in atonement for the execution of Louis XVI, and there was even talk of levelling Notre Dame. Pressure was growing to shoot the hostages, in revenge for Versaillais 'atrocities' at the front.

The arch enemy, Thiers, particularly drew Communard animosity – one ferocious cartoon depicting him in the act of unnatural relations with Bismarck. Suddenly, guided by the demagogue de Rochefort, the Jacobins realised they held a card for striking a cruel blow at the hated Thiers in person. In Paris Thiers owned a superb house, filled with art treasures and priceless books, which was his pride and joy. The Committee of Public Safety now decreed that this house should be 'razed to the ground' and its contents confiscated. On 15 May sentence was carried out. It was, said Edwin Child, present at the demolition, 'as striking an instance of futile spite, as perhaps any revolution can or has to furnish'.

Moderate Parisians now began to dread where the Commune's next excesses would lead. In particular, the life of the Archbishop was clearly in the gravest jeopardy. So far, protected as long as he remained a valuable pawn to trade against Blanqui, he had seemed safe. Minister Washburne had recently gained permission to visit him. Taking him 'a bottle of old Madeira and some newspapers', Washburne found him in a gloomy cell, six feet by ten, such as housed common felons; bearded, 'his face haggard with ill-health . . . he seemed to appreciate his critical position, and to be prepared for the worst . . .'

After his visit, Washburne pressed Thiers again to accept Rigault's offer to exchange the Archbishop for Blanqui, on the grounds 'that I considered him in the most imminent danger . . .' Thiers more or less told Washburne to mind his own business. As rebels, the Communards could expect none of the privileges of real warfare, and he would have no dealings with them. On 19 May Washburne visited Monseigneur Darboy again, bringing him this bad news: 'I found him very feeble. He has been confined to his pallet for the last week with a kind of pleurisy; is without appetite, and very much reduced in strength,' Washburne reported to Secretary of State Fish. It was to be his final meeting with the doomed Archbishop.

That same day Rigault initiated the summary 'Juries of Accusation'. The hostages were divided into two categories, the first of which included the Archbishop and the remainder of the imprisoned priests. The second category, the small fry of Second Empire policemen, were dealt with first and, after a trial lasting a few hours, were returned to prison to await their fate as hostages. The trial of the Archbishop was fixed for the following week, but events overtook it.

Rigault in his zeal, however, had been arresting the wrong hostages. By far the best one in the hands of the Commune was the Bank of France, still untouched: 'Through it they held the genital organs of Versailles . . .'

Instead, on 16 May – 26 Floréal – the Jacobin Communards embarked on one of their most memorable, as well as futile, acts. The Vendôme Column had been erected by Napoleon I in emulation of Trajan's masterpiece in Rome, with bronze bas-reliefs (cast from melted-down enemy cannon) to celebrate the victories of 1805 winding for 840 feet upwards around the column. At its summit stood a massive effigy of the Emperor, clad in toga and laurel wreath. Under the Second Empire, the Column had represented to even the moderate Leftists all they most detested about militarism and imperialism. Back in September 1870, the boozy and somewhat inflated Courbet (who claimed an additional motive in that the Column was aesthetically offensive to his professional eye) had been urging Trochu

Bourgœis inspecting the body of a Communard

Louis-Charles
Delescluze

General de Gallifet – scourge of the Commune

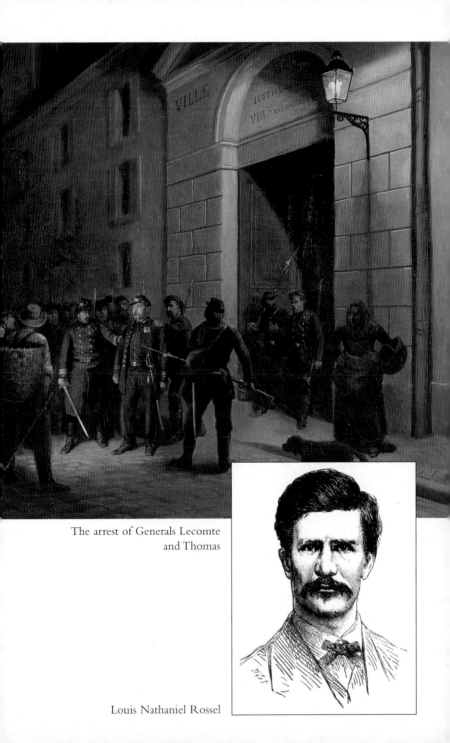

The arrest of Generals Lecomte
and Thomas

Louis Nathaniel Rossel

Cannon on the Buttes-Montmartre on the eve of 18 March 1871

The arrest of Louise Michel

Execution of Communards at Père Lachaise Cemetery

The execution of a trumpeter from a painting by Alfred Roll

to have it demolished. Now at last the Commune had acceded to Courbet's desires, with the Jacobins pressing for immediate action. But it was not easy, technically, to bring down this massive shaft, 155 feet high and immensely thick.

After several failures, the successful applicant for the job was discovered (according to Goncourt) in the shape of an engineer with a demanding mistress who had been racking his brain for ways of making easy money. He produced the idea of felling the column like some gigantic tree, and was paid 6,000 francs (promptly passed on to his *amourette*) for his brainwave. Workmen began laboriously to hew through the bronze and stone. The day appointed for the felling was to be the biggest festivity since the Commune was proclaimed on 28 March. Battalions and bands of the National Guard were packed within the Place Vendôme (already renamed Place Internationale), transforming it into a dense mass of red scarves and gold braid. The *pavé* was covered with tons of manure and straw; it would never do if the falling column went straight through into the sewers. Capstans had been installed with ropes attached to the top of the column. All that now remained was to winch the capstans and pull it over.

At 3 p.m. on 26 Floréal, the bands struck up the *Marseillaise*, and the capstans began to strain. But after half-an-hour's tugging, a snatch-block broke, injuring several men. There were cries of 'Treason', and the bands tried to divert the impatient crowds with patriotic airs; during which time navvies hacked their way deeper into the great gouge in the column. An extra fifty men pulled on the ropes, and by 6 p.m. the great column started to lean. Suddenly, with a shattering crash, it 'lay on the ground, a huge mass of ruin. An immense dust and smoke from the stones and crumpled clay rose up, and an instant after a crowd of men, National Guards, Commune, and sight-seeing English flew upon it, and commenced to get bits of it as remembrance . . .'

A tremendous clamour broke out. Amid roars of '*Vive la Commune!*' Communard leaders attempted to make the customary speeches, which nobody could hear, from the stump of the column. Other members of the crowd rushed up to spit on the remains of the great Emperor, broken and fallen in the dust. As an additional reward, the amorous engineer received the little statue of Liberty held in Napoleon's hand.

Doubtless the Jacobins hoped that the spectacle would distract minds from the grim realities beyond the walls of Paris. Thiers's men were drawing ever closer. Following the fall of Fort Issy, just north of the Point du Jour salient on which Thiers had his eyes fixed, General Clinchant was digging parallels across the Bois de Boulogne almost up to the Porte de la Muette. The city itself was now directly menaced.

Meanwhile, life for civilians in Paris became more and more hazardous. Inhabitants of the fashionable '*Seizième*' at Passy found themselves caught under cannon fire from both sides: 'This morning the guns established at the Trocadéro, endeavouring to hit the Bois de Boulogne, succeeded in landing their projectiles on the houses at the corner of Rue de la Pompe and La Tour [roughly midway]. . . . Bravo, bravo, they drink well, the Communard gunners, but aim badly!' wrote Jules Rafinesque.

'Strolling' up to the Trocadéro, Edwin Child noted that the Communards were barely able to reply any longer to the intense Government bombardment; 'most of their pieces being dismounted, and they altogether are becoming fast demoralised so that an end appears not far distant'.

Yet still, despite the menace hanging over the city, in that remarkable Parisian way life in its more superficial aspects seemed to continue unaffected. Still the Seine fishermen stood as they had done during the First Siege, quiet and motionless, with rods held in unshaking hands as the cannon-balls whistled overhead. Labourers worked away in their allotments, while weight-lifters drew large crowds on the boulevards – 'a sight such as you might see on the green of a provincial village on a fête day'. Could anything ever stifle the irrepressible spring-time vivacity of Paris?

On 6 May, as Fort Issy was tottering, the Commune threw open the stately *Salle des Maréchaux* in the Tuileries Palace, where Louis-Napoleon's belles had once waltzed, for the first of a series of concerts to collect funds for the wounded. With them, an extraordinary kind of exaltation, almost of valedictory gaiety, seemed to seize the Communards as the final catastrophe became more obviously imminent. Each week the concerts were repeated, accompanied by the inevitable recitals of Victor Hugo's *Châtiments*, and culminating with singing of the hugely-applauded current hit: '*C'est la canaille, Eh! bien, j'en suis!*' (They're the rabble, Ah well! I'm one of them.')

But the most grandiose concert, with fifteen hundred musicians participating, was the one that took place on the evening of Sunday, 21 May. At its end, a Communard officer rose to announce: 'Citizens, M. Thiers promised to enter Paris yesterday. M. Thiers did not enter; he will not enter. Therefore I invite you here next Sunday, here at this same place . . .'

There were wild cheers. At that precise moment, however, the troops of M. Thiers were beginning to pour into the city.

Since 13 May, hopes had been roused in the Government camp that a loyal Fifth Columnist would open one of the western gates of the city. Some eighty thousand men were standing by, concealed in the Bois de Boulogne. Every succeeding day an impatient Thiers had visited this front. But nothing had happened. Then, on Sunday the 21st, just as he was resignedly ordering a Council of War to plan a general assault on the walls, a white flag was seen fluttering close to the Point du Jour Gate. Waving it was a civil engineer named Ducatel, who felt no love for the Commune and who had happened quite by chance to stroll near the battlements on his afternoon promenade. He was astonished to perceive that, around the Point du Jour, which had been heavily pounded by Thiers's cannon over the past few days, there was not a defender to be seen. With alacrity he mounted the ramparts and signalled to the waiting army. A Versailles major came forward, soon verifying Ducatel's discovery.

When Thiers reached the scene, he saw 'two long black serpents, winding through folds in the ground, and heading

— 19 —

BLOODY WEEK

At the Hôtel de Ville, the Commune was busy with its last legislation. In the past four days new decrees had been passed on Legitimacy, on the Secularisation of Education, on theatres; while another order had sent some staff officers, caught phil-andering with *cocottes*, to the front with picks and shovels (the girls to a sandbag factory). Now the Assembly was in the midst of judging the fallen Cluseret. Suddenly (it was about 7 o'clock on Sunday evening, the 21st) a wild-eyed official burst in, demanded an immediate secret session, and then read out a dispatch from Dombrowski reporting the Versailles entry. There was 'a stupefied silence' followed by uproar, Rigault at once proposing they blow up the Seine bridges, and withdraw to conduct a last-ditch defence in his old hunting ground, the Quartier Latin, burning all behind them. The hostages were to be brought along too, 'and they will perish there with us'.

A haggard Delescluze received the news grimly at the Min-istry of War, then dictated a street-by-street defence of the city, placing Brunel – just released from a second spell in prison the previous night – in command of the key position around the Place de la Concorde. Finally he issued a rousing proclamation to the Citizens of Paris: 'Enough of militarism! No more Gen-eral Staffs with badges of rank and gold braid at every seam! Make way for the people, for the fighters with bare arms! The hour of revolutionary warfare has struck!'

It was a call to the barricades, and the old appeal for the spon-taneous, unorganised, torrential *levée en masse* heard so often from Delescluze and the Reds during the First Siege. But none

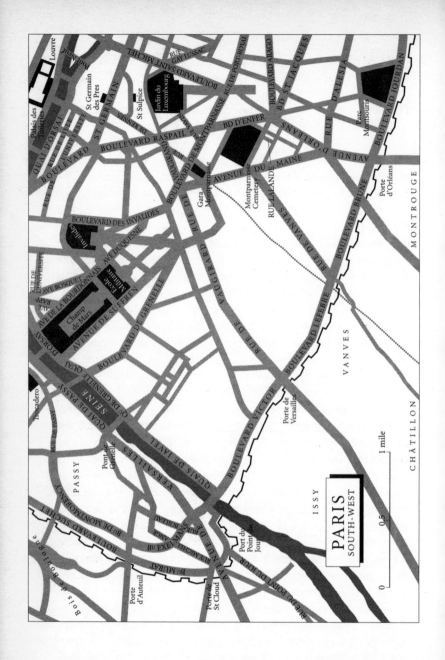

of the second line of barricades prescribed by Rossel had been completed, and now there would be no coherent plan of defence either. At 5 a.m., leaving all his papers undestroyed, Delescluze abandoned his office and set off for the barricades.

That night Goncourt heard rumours of Thiers's entry, then returned home. Unable to sleep, 'I seemed to be able to hear a confused murmur in the distance. In a street some way off there was the usual noise of one company relieving another, as happened every night. I told myself I had been imagining things and went back to bed . . . but this time there was no mistaking the sound of drum and bugle! I rushed back to the window. The call to arms was sounding all over Paris, and soon, drowning the noise of the drums and the bugles and the shouting and the cries of "To Arms!" came the great, tragic, booming notes of the tocsin being rung in all the churches – a sinister sound which filled me with joy and sounded the death-knell of the odious tyranny oppressing Paris.'

Paul Verlaine, employed by the Commune press office, was awakened by the voice of his wife dreaming aloud that the Versaillais had entered Paris. Then the maid came in to tell her it was no dream, and Madame Verlaine at once packed to take refuge with her parents.

It was not until Monday morning that most Parisians learned the news. At Auteuil, Dombrowski's forces had been taken completely by surprise. There had been a desperate but brief defence on the line of the Ceinture railway; then panic. A major come from the lost ramparts assured Dombrowski that he had beaten his fleeing troops 'with the flat of his sword till his arm ached; but he could not stay the panic'. Without losing his head, Dombrowski dispatched an urgent request to Delescluze for reinforcements. But MacMahon's troops, advancing through the friendly territory of Passy, had already made remarkably rapid initial progress.

Sent on a reconnaissance, Assi, the incompetent first Chairman of the Commune, was captured near the Trocadéro – the first of the Commune leaders to be taken. By dawn MacMahon had already poured 70,000 troops through five gaping breaches

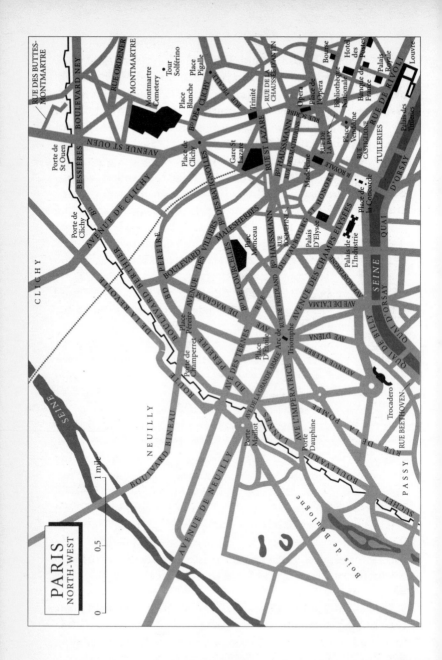

in the walls between the Porte de Passy and the Porte St-Cloud, and some 1,500 National Guards had surrendered. The whole of Auteuil and Passy had been 'liberated', as well as most of the 15th Arrondissement on the other side of the Seine. Residents like the Rafinesque family were almost overcome with joy and gratitude towards the Versailles Army.

A frenzy of desperate energy now seized the Commune. At bayonet-point passing citizens were everywhere forced to assist build the barricades that should have been completed weeks ago: 'If possible two or three trolleys, cabs or carts would form the foundation; all the apertures being filled with sand, the cubic paving stones from the road, sandbags, bricks or anything else . . . in such wide streets as the Rue Royale, the barricade was made by engineers, and were small fortresses with place for cannon, and very strong.'

But vast numbers of Parisians who had ardently backed the Commune in its earliest days unostentatiously 'vanished', so as to avoid building barricades and escape impressment. Thus did the Commune's marginal supporters fade away in its hour of need. Others simply went to ground until it was all over. Goncourt found refuge with Burty, the art critic, near the Bibliothèque Nationale: 'I buried myself in his Delacroix to the sound of exploding shells coming gradually nearer.'

By the end of the morning, General Douay's men had seized the heavily sand-bagged Arc de Triomphe. Their cannon could now sweep all the way down the Champs-Elysées, only so recently crammed with gay, festive crowds. So far the Versaillais had encountered practically no opposition, and were full of confidence. But all of a sudden concentrated volleys of fire flashed out from the terrace of the Tuileries Gardens. Struck at point-blank range and caught thoroughly off balance, the lead-ing Versaillais suffered heavy losses; the survivors fled back as far as the Palais de l'Industrie. The advance had received its first check, administered by the tough and competent Brunel, and for the rest of the day Douay's force consolidated around the Étoile. Washburne at the American Legation, now in

Government-held territory, found himself once again under shell-fire, this time from Communard guns.

On the Left Bank, Communards fought at Montparnasse Station until ammunition ran out; then their withdrawal was covered by a courageous singleton, who kept up a steady fire into the station from a one-man stronghold inside a newspaper kiosk. At the other end of the front, the Versailles troops were advancing rapidly towards Montmartre, having captured the Parc Monceau when National Guards directed a murderous fire into the rear of their own front-line defenders, mistaking them for Versaillais.

Living just behind the Madeleine, an English doctor, Alan Herbert, soon found himself a fascinated spectator of the Communard defence as, with mounting ferocity, Frenchmen killed Frenchmen: 'The first who fired was a grey-headed, grey-bearded old man, who was the most blood-thirsty old fellow I ever saw. He hounded the others on . . . it was a horrible sight. They quarrelled as to . . . whose turn it was to shoot, and from time to time one heard such expressions as these: "Oh, that caught him!" It was just like boys rabbit-shooting. I do not believe, however, they *killed* many . . .'

Inside the Hôtel de Ville something of the heat, confusion and excitement of the March days had been recaptured. All the various organs of the Commune had assembled here, and were busy issuing contradictory orders. Pyat was there, declaring theatrically 'our last hour has come'. He was distressed to see all those young men about to die, but 'for me, what does it matter! My hair is white, my career is finished. What more glorious end could I hope for than to die on the barricades!' To prove to posterity, that he, Félix Pyat, had done his duty he now called for a roll-call of all those present. Then, in his familiar fashion, he disappeared. His white hair was not seen on any barricade – in fact, not seen again at all until Pyat turned up safely in exile in London.

Little of sense was being transmitted from the Hôtel de Ville by way of military instructions for the hard-pressed National Guard. Haussmann's layout of the new Paris was proving – as intended – admirable for the regular troops to execute turning movements on the Communard barricades. A co-ordinated, mobile defence might have coped with these tactics; but there was no longer a Rossel, or even a Cluseret, to dispose of the Commune's forces.

Late on Monday night, Dombrowski was brought under arrest to the Hôtel de Ville. Without a command since that morning, he had been seized (so it was claimed) while trying to flee the city. The Pole vigorously denied contemplating treason. The Committee of Public Safety 'appeased him affectionately'; Dombrowski strode off grimly towards the fighting.

About the only Government advance that afternoon had been to capture the garden of the British Embassy on the Rue St-Honoré. In their scattered little packets, the Communards were beginning to fight as never before – the fight of despair. As the front stabilised by nightfall, it lay roughly along a north-south axis, running from the Gare des Batignolles in the north, through the Gare St-Lazare, the British Embassy, the Palais de l'Industrie, across the Seine to the Chamber of Deputies, and up the Boulevard des Invalides to the Gare Montparnasse. Behind it, on the one side, the western third of Paris lay solidly in Government hands.

To a jubilant Assembly at Versailles, Thiers announced that 'the cause of justice, order, humanity, civilisation has triumphed. . . . The generals who conducted the entry into Paris are great men of war.' Thiers added ominously: 'Expiation will be complete. It will take place in the name of the law, by the law and within the law.'

In the final judgement of Paris that lay immediately ahead, it might be possible to perceive 'order'; but remarkably little of justice, humanity or civilisation.

The dawn of Tuesday the 23rd broke on another ravishing May day. Ladmirault and Clinchant were already assaulting the bastion of Montmartre from two directions. The defence presented a dismal spectacle of discouragement, half-completed barricades and unserviceable guns. Many of the defenders had faded away during the night, leaving only a hundred or so men to man the defences on the northern slopes upon which Ladmirault was advancing with more than a division. About the only Communard detachment which showed spirit was a squad of twenty-five women from the Women's Battalion, headed by the redoubtable Louise Michel. Back along the Boulevard de Clichy they fought from barricade to barricade; past the Place Blanche, past the site of some of the more sordid night-haunts of modern Paris, back to the Place Pigalle, where most of them were forced to surrender. By this time only about fifteen of the women were left, including Louise Michel and Elizabeth Dimitrieff. Louise had orders to blow up, if necessary, the Butte Montmartre. But it was too late. Near the Boulevard Barbès she met Dombrowski, falling back from Clignancourt, at about two o'clock that afternoon. 'We are lost!' he told her, and a few seconds later he fell mortally wounded. Though so recently in disgrace, he was brought back to lie in state in a blue satin bed in the Hôtel de Ville.

By 1 p.m., the *tricolore* had replaced the Red Flag on the Tour Solferino, where the insurrection had first broken out. Here, more than a hundred of the original cannon were recaptured, still disused. Now began the 'expiation' for which Thiers had called. Some forty-nine Communards were collected at random and summarily shot in the Rue des Rosiers, the site of the lynching of the two generals – among them, allegedly, seven women and children.

According to Dr Herbert, there were similar scenes when the Madeleine was taken that day: 'we saw the insurgents retreat from the different barricades and cross the Place. The troops then came in. A few scenes of horrid massacre and bloodshed, and then the streets were occupied by the regular troops. . . . I fear there is a very revengeful disposition amongst the regular troops, which is much to be regretted.'

Haussmann's still unfinished Opéra was soon hemmed in on three sides. Marine sharp-shooters mounted themselves in the top storey of the surrounding buildings, and directed a deadly fire down on to the Communards exposed behind their barricades; but here they fought back with desperate courage. At

6 p.m., after both sides had suffered substantial losses, the Opéra was carried; and a soldier climbed up on to the statue of Apollo at its entrance and ripped down the red flag.

Goncourt, browsing behind the Bibliothèque Nationale, now observed the signs of retreat begin to multiply. First horse-drawn ambulances, then, that evening, a horde of retreating National Guards came into sight, bearing with them 'a dead man with his head covered in blood, whom four men were carrying by his arms and legs like a bundle of dirty washing, taking him from door to door' – none of which were opened by the compassionate Parisians. Peeping through the curtain, Goncourt saw a Communard across the street killed by a bullet. His companion 'threw off his sword behind him, as if with scornful deliberation, bent down and tried to lift the dead man. The body was large and heavy, and, like any inert object, evaded his efforts and rolled about in his arms from left to right. At last he raised it; and clutching it across his chest, he was carrying it away when a bullet, smashing his thigh, made the dead and the living spin in a hideous pirouette, collapsing one upon the other. . . . I retained in my ear for a long time the rending cries of a wounded soldier who had dragged himself to our door and whom the concierge, through a cowardly fear of compromising herself, refused to let in.'

That night, away in the darkness, Parisians saw the red glow of a great fire. It looked as if the Tuileries Palace might be burning.

— 20 —

PARIS BURNS

All through Tuesday the 23rd, Brunel and his men had continued to hold out with the utmost tenacity at the barricades in the Rue Royale and the Place de la Concorde, and at the immensely strong one at the bottom of the Rue St-Florentin which guarded the Rue de Rivoli, the street pointing so straight at the Hôtel de Ville and the very heart of the Commune. Douay had brought no less than sixty guns to bear on Brunel's position, against a meagre twelve. Their concentrated fire reduced the barricades to a shambles, killing scores of the defenders. Turning movements from the direction of the Opéra were threatening their rear, and now deadly rifle-fire from sharpshooters on top of the high buildings along the Rue Royale mowed them down behind their barricades. Swiftly Brunel – justifying the nickname of 'The Burner' gained during the First Siege – ordered the firing of these buildings. With alarming speed the flames spread up the famous street, consuming expensive *bijouteries* and elegant cafés alike.

A month previously Henri Dunant, visiting the German lines, had been told by the Crown Prince of Saxony of an ancient prophecy that Paris would be burnt by its citizens in 1871. Now fulfilment of that prophecy had begun; it was to become as integral a part of the legend of the Commune as the rats and balloons of the First Siege. For 'Burner Brunel', however, the conflagration could only postpone the inevitable.

Falling back in desperate haste towards the Hôtel de Ville, Brunel and his men found their way lit by an immense fire that had broken out behind them. Bergeret, just released from prison, had carried out a desperate action, dictated, apparently, more by vengefulness than military necessity. Inside the Tuileries Palace, where only two days previously the last of the famous concerts had taken place, he piled barrel after barrel of gunpowder. With a tremendous roar the central dome housing the *Salle des Maréchaux* disappeared, dwarfing any firework display laid on by the former Emperor. Bergeret scribbled a note to the Committee of Public Safety: 'The last relics of Royalty have just vanished.' Even if it had not succeeded hitherto, the Commune was now certainly beginning to leave a permanent mark on the face of France.

The sounds of musketry were coming appreciably closer to the Hôtel de Ville. Corridors lit up by the diabolic glow from the Tuileries were cluttered with wounded, groaning for water, the walls flecked with their blood. Men's eyes now betrayed an awful fear, something beyond the transient panics of the past. In a temporary office, 'Delescluze is signing orders,' wrote Lissagaray 'pale, mute like a spectre. The agonies of the past days have drained what remained of his life. His voice is nothing but a croak.'

Without any authority from Delescluze, Raoul Rigault was meanwhile busy exacting his own vengeance. Arriving at Sainte Pelagie, he decreed the immediate execution of the first of the hostages, Gustave Chaudey, who had ordered the Mobiles to fire on the mob outside the Hôtel de Ville on 22 January. 'You killed my friend Sapia; you have five minutes to live,' Rigault told him. A reluctant firing squad merely wounded Chaudey, leaving it to the prison warders to finish off the job with revolvers. Next Rigault ordered out three wretched gendarmes, seized on 18 March. Only one was killed outright; another tried to escape, hiding like some hunted rodent in the shadows of the courtyard until dragged out and shot.

To Edwin Child lying low in the Marais, by the night of the 24th 'it seemed literally as if the whole town was on fire and as if all the powers of hell were let loose . . .' The list of buildings already incendiarised was appallingly impressive: the Tuileries, a large part of the Palais-Royal, the Palais de Justice, the

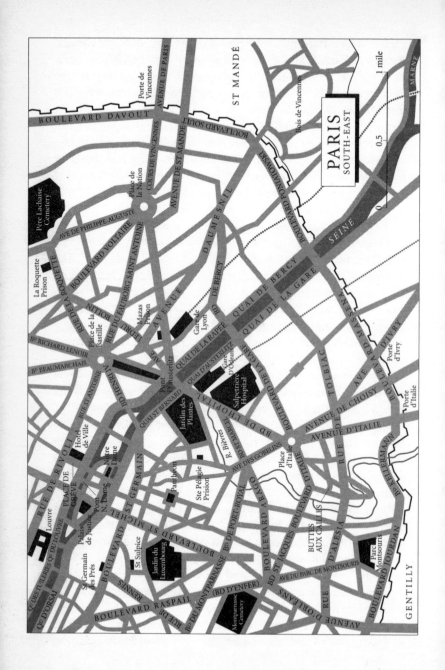

Prefecture of Police, the Legion d'Honneur, and the Conseil d'État. Whole sections of streets like the Rue de Lille and much of the Rue de Rivoli were ablaze; so was the Ministry of Finance, housed in one wing of the Louvre, and the priceless treasures in the Museum itself were gravely threatened. At Notre Dame, National Guards building up a large 'brazier' from chairs and pews were just forestalled in time. Evacuated by the desperate Commune, the superb medieval building of the Hôtel de Ville was also now consigned to the flames – despite the protests of Delescluze.

It was perfect weather for arson, the past month having been one of almost unbroken drought. Amid frantic attempts by the Government forces to stem the flames, rumours ran round that the Commune was planning to raze the whole of Paris. The *pétroleuses* entered the limelight, fearful maenads from some infernal region who allegedly crept about the city, flinging Molotov cocktails into basement windows belonging to the bourgeoisie. 'Last night,' wrote a Briton in Paris on 25 May, 'three women were caught throwing small fire balls down the openings of cellars in the street. There was no doubt of it of course. Already smoke was coming from some of them. They were driven into a corner and shot then and there through the head.'

The origin of the *pétroleuses* remains a mystery. Possibly it was based on one genuine incident; but no serious evidence was ever produced in court, as most of the wretched women seized were shot out of hand – and how many innocent old crones met their deaths while returning empty bottles to the *laitière* will never be known. As the blood of kith and kin flowed in growing streams, atrocity was followed by reprisal and counter-reprisal. To Secretary of State Fish, Washburne reported: 'The state of feeling now existing in Paris is fearful beyond description.'

That night the Communards committed their most infamous crime. The imprisoned Archbishop and fifty other hostages had been recently transferred to the more secure prison of La Roquette, in the heart of Red Paris. In charge of them was

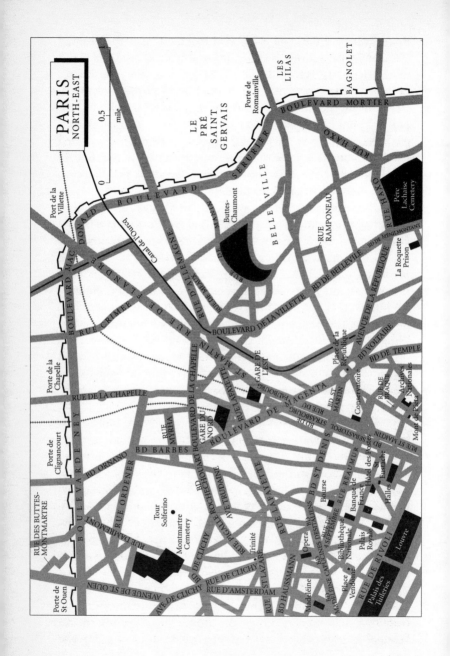

Rigault's new Prefect of Police, Théophile Ferré. A dedicated terrorist of twenty-five, Ferré had a shock of black hair and whiskers that surrounded a bird-of-prey face of extraordinary pallor and melancholy. On his great hooked nose sat thick glasses through which peered black eyes full of all the myopic mildness of a Himmler. With deformedly short legs, he walked on tiptoe with a nervous tic of the shoulder. Nature had indeed provided him with a warrantable grudge against the world.

Enraged by news of fresh Versailles atrocities, a 'Red' mob pressed Ferré for the execution of the hostages. He needed little persuasion. Together with five other priests, the Archbishop – evidently showing great courage, though much weakened by illness – was led out into an alley. The National Guards' aim was as inaccurate as ever, and several volleys had to be fired. They then ripped open the Archbishop's body with their bayonets, and carried it off to be thrown into an open ditch at Père Lachaise cemetery. When Delescluze was told of the death of the Archbishop, he buried his face in his hands and groaned: 'What a war! What a war!'

Retribution was not long delayed in catching up with Rigault. The next day he was seized on the Left Bank, at lodgings he shared under an assumed name with an actress. Shot in the head, for two days the Procureur's body lay in the gutter, partly stripped by women of the district and kicked and spat upon by passers-by.

By evening on the 24th, the fighting on the Left Bank had all but come to an end. For two terrible days Varlin and Lisbonne had put up a spirited defence, then withdrawn, blowing up the huge powder magazine at the Luxembourg. The Versaillais followed closely, shooting surrendered Communards in batches as they went, but Varlin escaped across the river, still fighting. Only Wroblewski was left, holding out for another day in a stronghold near the Porte d'Italie with something of the suicidal courage that evokes the Warsaw rising of 1944.

On the Right Bank, only the eastern corner of Paris still remained in Communard hands. One by one the leaders were falling. A wounded Frankel came back from the Bastille supported by Elizabeth Dimitrieff, herself wounded. Lisbonne was badly hit; 'Burner' Brunel was crippled with a bullet in the thigh, but young boys of his 'Youth Battalion' loyally bore him off to safety. Looking more than ever like a man under imminent sentence of death, Delescluze hurried from barricade to barricade, supervising, encouraging, exhorting. On the evening of the 25th, he sat down to write a farewell letter to his sister: 'I no longer feel I possess the courage,' he said, 'to submit to another defeat, after so many others.' Then, dressed as always like an 1848 revolutionary in a top hat, polished boots, black trousers and frock coat, a red sash around his waist and leaning heavily on a cane, he set off towards an abandoned barricade. Lissagaray saw him slowly, painfully clamber up to the top; then pitch forward on his face. In defeat, the old Jacobin had achieved a certain nobility denied to either the Emperor at Sedan, or Ducrot at the Great Sortie.

The Commune was now leaderless.

Friday 26 May was a day of savage killings on both sides, in which the battle became a mopping-up operation. It was also the day the rains came, mercifully. The blaze in the Ministry of Finance was extinguished, and by a very narrow margin indeed the Louvre was saved. But rain could not quench the rage and hatred which had built up in the conquering army.

The dejected columns of prisoners marching westwards through Paris, guarded by General Gallifet's cavalry, were growing ever longer. Even the rabid anti-Communard, Goncourt, was moved to pity by the sight of them: 'The men had been split up into lines of seven or eight and tied to each other with string that cut into their wrists. They were just as they had been captured, most of them without hats or caps, and with their hair plastered down on their foreheads and faces by the fine rain that had been falling ever since this morning. There were men of the people there who had made themselves head coverings out of blue check handkerchiefs. Others, drenched to the skin by the rain, were carrying a hunk of bread.'

Many never reached Versailles. Before Alphonse Daudet's eyes: 'A large man, a true southerner, sweating, panting, had difficulty in keeping up. Two cavalrymen came up, attached tethers to each of his arms, around his body, and galloped. The man tries to run, but falls; he is dragged, a mass of bleeding flesh that emits a croaking sound; murmurs of pity from the crowd: "Shoot him, and have done!" One of the troopers halts his horse, comes up and fires his carbine into the moaning and kicking parcel of meat. He is not dead . . . the other trooper jumps from his horse, fires again. This time, that's it.'

On the edge of the Bois de Boulogne, the Marquis de Gallifet – sparkling gallant of Second Empire days, and hero of Sedan – set up his own 'sifting' process, thereby gaining a reputation for ferocity that Paris would never forget. 'I am Gallifet,' he told prisoners. 'You people of Montmartre may think me cruel, but I am even crueller than you can imagine.' It was no idle boast. Arbitrarily, Communards with grey hair were singled out, on the assumption that they must also have fought on the barricades of '48; those with watches as possible 'officials' of the Commune; while any Communard found to have been formerly a regular soldier was automatically marched off for execution.

The Communards responded with new savagery. Fifty more of the remaining hostages, gendarmes and priests, were taken out from La Roquette, accompanied by a terrible escort of drunk and jeering rabble, to a point so close to the city walls that they could hear snatches of waltz music being played on German accordions, on the other side. At the risk of his own life, Varlin tried to intercede, but in vain. No proper firing squad was constituted; instead a hideous, uncoordinated butchery took place, with anyone who had a weapon firing it into the huddled group of hostages.

On Saturday the 27th, the arrival at La Roquette of the dreaded Ferré drove the surviving hostages beyond the threshold of terror, and they frantically rushed up their own barricades. Unable to force an entry, an execution squad tried to smoke them out with burning mattresses. But the hostages fought back with a despair only equalled by the Communards dying on the last barricades outside.

Belleville and Menilmontant alone were still wholly in

Communard hands. Here, as at Warsaw and Leningrad in the Second World War, a whole population was now fighting. Every man, woman and child was ready to serve and die on the barricades; and, knowing that they could now expect no quarter, they were fighting with all the despair of trapped animals.

Vinoy's regulars were approaching the last of the Commune's remaining strongholds: Père Lachaise cemetery. Possessing what is still one of the best views in Paris, the vast cemetery dominated the whole smouldering city. It was defended by two batteries of guns and some two hundred National Guards. Amid the massive family vaults of the *deux cent familles* and the less imposing tombs of France's famous poets, painters and musicians a dreadful carnage ensued. Bullets splintered the marble and granite; blood sullied pretentious gravestones in this macabre battlefield. Finally, in hand-to-hand combat the last defender was winkled out near Balzac's tomb.

The Belleville Mairie – the terminal headquarters of the Commune – had become a refuge for untended wounded, hysterical women and whimpering, terrified children, but soon this too fell to Government forces. Then they liberated the hostages at La Roquette, still holding out, surrounded by a howling mob.

Fifteen miles outside Paris, Daudet hearing the rumbling of the cannon was reminded of 'a great ship in distress'. 'I felt that the Commune, about to go down, was firing its last distress rockets. At every minute I could see the wreck heave up, the breach in it grow bigger, and then inside I could see the men of the Hôtel de Ville clinging to their stage, and continuing to decree and decree amid all the din of the wind and the tempest.'

The next morning, 28 May, Thiers's army moved in for the kill. It was Whit Sunday. For a whole week the Commune had fought back against enormous odds, but now all was over. Led by Varlin, the last survivors were hemmed into a tiny square fragment of Paris. In a few hours, there was only one barricade left, in the Rue Ramponneau. Here, a solitary unknown defender held off the attackers with a cool and deadly aim; having fired off his last cartridge, he strolled calmly away and disappeared.

His hands bound behind his back, Varlin was dragged up to Montmartre, beaten with rifle butts all along the way, and half lynched by jeering crowds of Parisians. By the time he reached the sinister Rue des Rosiers, which had become a regular 'expiation' centre, his face was a pulp and one eye was dangling out of its socket. No longer able to stand, he was carried out into the garden, to be shot seated in a chair.

At Père Lachaise cemetery Vinoy's troops had found the unburied corpse of the murdered Archbishop. That Whitsun morning they marched 147 of the captured Communards out to the cemetery, lined them up against a wall in its eastern corner, and mowed them down.

The 'expiation' promised by Thiers now began in earnest. An orgy of killing took place. Many innocents were killed in mistake for Communard leaders; at least two 'Burner' Brunels were reported shot, while the real one was on his way to enjoy a ripe old age in England. Chimneysweeps were executed, on the assumption that their hands had been blackened by gunpowder, not soot. Inside La Roquette, with such grim memories for the hostages of the Commune, some 1,900 prisoners are said to have been shot in two days, and at the Mazas prison another 400. All night waggons clattered through the streets, occupied in the gruesome task of disposing of the corpses.

Those lucky enough to reach Versailles were crammed into Black Holes of Calcutta called 'reception centres'. Kept short of water, food and medical attention, a number died of suffocation. Here too the shootings went on.

Repugnance at what was happening in the *ville lumière* began to make its impact abroad. On 1 June, *The Times* declared: 'Human nature shrinks in horror from the deeds that have been done in Paris. . . . The wholesale executions inflicted by the Versailles soldiery, the triumph, the glee, the ribaldry of the "Party of Order", sicken the soul.'

Even France herself was sickening of the slaughter. 'Let us kill no more, even murderers and incendiaries!' the *Paris-Journal* implored on 2 June. 'Let us kill no more!'

THAT LITTLE FLAME

'What a sight met my eyes!' exclaimed Edwin Child as he emerged from his refuge at the end of the fighting. 'Destruction everywhere. From the Châtelet to Hôtel de Ville, all was destroyed, not a room left . . .' The city indeed presented a terrible spectacle. The Tritons in the fountains of the Place de la Concorde were twisted into fantastic shapes, the statue of Lille decapitated. Gautier, revisiting the Rue de Lille, said it 'seemed to be deserted throughout its length, like a street of Pompeii'. Of Prosper Merimée's old house there, nothing remained but the walls: 'A silence of death reigned over these ruins; in the necropolises of Thebes or in the shafts of the Pyramids it was no more profound. No clatter of vehicles, no shouts of children, not even the song of a bird. . . . An incurable sadness invaded our souls . . .'

Yet more had survived than people thought possible. The Venus de Milo was brought forth from her hiding-place in the incendiarised Prefecture de Police, where by a miracle a burst water pipe had apparently preserved the packing-case in which she lay. As she was removed from her 'coffin', said Gautier, 'everybody leaned forward avidly to contemplate her. She still smiled, lying there so softly . . . this vague and tender smile, her lips slightly apart as if all the better to breathe in life . . .'

It seemed like a symbol of the return of life to Paris herself. With astonishing speed that summer omnibuses and *fiacres* were plying the streets again, *bateaux-mouches* bustling up and down the Seine. Even the enterprising Thomas Cook was sending hordes of English tourists to goggle at the 'ruins' of Paris. For some time the sale of petroleum and all inflammable products was banned, and cafés were required to close by 11 p.m., but on 3 June the theatre doors reopened.

In 1873 the National Assembly voted the erection of an immense basilica – 'in witness of repentance and as a symbol of hope' – to be called the Sacré-Cœur, and to be at Montmartre on the spot where the insurrection had started. There was much to be repented. Estimates of the numbers of Parisians slaughtered during and following *la semaine sanglante* vary wildly between 6,500 and 40,000. Reliable French historians today seem more or less agreed on a figure of between 20,000 and 25,000. In any event, the total is still staggering. No single battle of the Franco-Prussian War cost so many lives; nor did the whole duration of the Terror in the Great Revolution; nor, even, did Lenin's October Revolution of 1917 in St Petersburg. And all this had taken place not in some remote African territory, nor by the whim of some long-dead Oriental despot, but in a recent age perhaps rather more humanitarian than our own; and in a city which regarded itself as *the* Citadel of Civilisation.

Justice continued to be apportioned among the 40,000 Communard prisoners until 1875. Ferré and Rossel were executed – the latter's sentence a source of much heart-rending among patriotic Frenchmen, but it was his background as a senior officer of the regular army, as well as the brash threat he had issued to the would-be captor of Fort Issy, that doomed Rossel's. 251 rebels were sentenced to forced labour for life, including Urbain, the author of the 'Hostages Decree'. Another 4,500 were transported, either to waste away in a fortress or in exile under dreadful conditions in some grim colony. Among these numbered Rochefort and Louise Michel. Courbet (if ever there was a case of punishment fitting the crime) was ordered to pay up to 250,000 francs towards the reconstruction of the Vendôme Column, but rather than find this astronomic sum of money he fled to Switzerland.

An astonishing number of other leading Communards also escaped Thiers's net. Bergeret, condemned to death *in absentia*, found refuge in the United States. Cluseret, who, pending trial had taken no part in the fighting for Paris, left Paris disguised as a priest, and (unsuccessfully) claimed American protection. Wandering in exile through Switzerland, Turkey, Britain and the USA, he eventually returned to France after the amnesty to be elected to the Assembly. Recovering from her wounds, the beautiful Dimitrieff reached Switzerland, finally marrying a Russian exile in Siberia, where she died. Many Communards found refuge in London. Longuet and Lafarge each married one of Marx's daughters; Pyat fulminated there, until amnesty allowed him to return to France where he became a somewhat risible adornment of the Senate. After serving her time on Noumea, Louise Michel also returned to France; still a violent anarchist, she was arrested several times more before having to flee to London, where she died in 1905 – exultant at the news of revolution in Russia.

Probably none of the Communards migrating to England had a more remarkable career than 'Burner' Brunel. Though badly wounded, he escaped from Paris (and a death sentence) and four years later found employment teaching French at the Royal Naval College, Dartmouth, until he died in 1904. Among his pupils was the future King George V.

The killings of 1871, the ensuing banishments and voluntary exiles, changed the face of Paris in a curious way. Half the house-painters, the plumbers, the tile-makers, shoe-makers, and zinc-workers had disappeared. In Belleville there were sullen streets which seemed to be tenanted solely by old women. Paris industry was hamstrung for some years.

Once Paris did recover, France herself was not far behind. After sketching dead Communards at the barricades, Manet was back at Boulogne painting *La Partie de Croquet*. Renoir and Degas came back to find studios in Paris; Monet and Pissarro returned from refuge in London. Suddenly, as if in reaction against the grim drabness and the horrors of the Siege and the Commune, the Impressionists burst forth into a new, passion- ate, glorious blaze of colour, redolent with the love of simple, ordinary existence. France had come back to life again. Her industry blossomed forth in a new renaissance. With totally unexpected rapidity, France paid up the crushing reparations bill to Germany; but she would never, never write off Alsace-Lorraine.

France's military defeat by Prussia upset the whole balance of power as it had existed in Europe since the downfall of the first Napoleon; the Commune, however, was to achieve more than that. For all the ephemeral, and so often foolish, content of its acts, the image of the Commune would linger long, and potently. Above all others, Karl Marx was determined that – despite his initial misgivings – this image should not fade. As early as April he was writing prophetically to his friend Kugelmann: 'The struggle of the working class against the capitalist class and its state has entered upon a new phase with the struggle in Paris. Whatever the immediate results may be, a new point of departure of world-historic importance has been gained.'

Out of the fabric of the Commune Marx was to weave social and revolutionary myths of immense portent. Within a matter of days, he had written *The Civil War in France*, next to the *Communist Manifesto* probably the most powerful tract he ever wrote, as well as being a remarkable *tour de force* of up-to-the-minute journalism.

Overnight Marx achieved a new universal notoriety as the 'Red Terrorist Doctor'. But his support for the Commune split the International down the centre; one side leading indirectly to the birth of the moderate British Labour Party; the other to Lenin's extremist Bolsheviks. He had succeeded, however, in creating a heroic Socialist legend. Still to this day, the Mur des Fédérés where the 147 Communard 'martyrs' were shot down at Père Lachaise is a Mecca for mass Left-wing pilgrimages every Whitsun.

For France, the Commune achieved at least one sacred cause; there could now be no question of risking substitution of the Republic by any kind of monarchist restoration. But, as Marx predicted, henceforth there could also 'be neither peace nor truce possible between the working men of France and the appropriators of their produce . . . the battle must break out again and again in ever-growing dimensions.' As a result bitterness was to be injected into French politics – still not exorcised today – beyond anything experienced in Britain or America. From the martyrdom of 1871 was to spring the Front Populaire of the 1930s, which so rent France, leaving her once again an easy prey to a new German menace.

But it was through Lenin that the Commune and Marx's interpretation of it was to have the most cosmic effect. All through his life Lenin studied the Commune: worshipped its heroism, analysed its successes, criticised its faults, and compared its failures with the failure of the abortive Russian revolution of 1905.

The Commune's half-measures in not marching on Versailles, not seizing the Bank of France, not smashing at once the existing politico-social order, taught Lenin an indispensable lesson in ruthlessness. When, on the eve of success in 1917, he was forced to flee briefly to Finland, Marx's *The Civil War in France* was one of the two books he took with him on his final exile. When he returned, it was to impose Communism upon Russia by means of a revolution that never would have succeeded had it not been for the 'dummy run' attempted by Delescluze and his martyrs. Constantly obsessed with fears that the October Revolution would go the same way, Lenin is said to have counted 'Commune plus one' each day it outlived the Commune.

When Lenin died, his body was appropriately shrouded in a Communard flag, and his mantle passed to Stalin. Once describing the Commune as 'an incomplete and fragile dictatorship', Stalin made sure that this charge would never be levelled against his pitiless brand of despotism.

After Stalin, in the Marxist hagiology the men of 1871 still retained a position of high eminence. When the first Soviet *Voskhod* headed for space in 1964, it was a shred off a Communard banner that was one of the principal *penates* it carried aloft.

EPILOGUE

At the time of its centenary in 1971, the Commune seemed to excite new sources of inspiration among the Left all over the world. Its theories impressed Chairman Mao; during the 'Cultural Revolution', apparently sparked from above, a 'Commune' was set up briefly at Shanghai in 1967, in the manifest hopes that the rest of China would follow its example. The following year, the *événements* in Paris bore obvious – and alarming – resemblance to moments of 1871, and once again the cries of *Vive la Commune!* were heard on the Left Bank of Paris. It was perhaps less obvious that the same slogan should also have become the favourite of rioting Tokyo students – seeking the kind of autonomy that some Parisians had hoped the Commune would grant Paris.

But since then, with the fall of the Soviets, Karl Marx has fallen on hard times – his message carried on notably by a few disgruntled standard-bearers of 'politically correct' at Oxford and other western universities.

How, in 2004, may one judge the Communards? As blood-thirsty cut-throats? Or as heroic martyrs of the proletarian vanguard? Or as precursors of 9/11, and the suicide bombers of the twenty-first century? Over the past century and a half, in France at any rate, it was often hard to find any moderate view between the two extremes.

'They were madmen', said Auguste Renoir, who narrowly escaped death at Communard hands as a young painter, 'but they had in them that little flame which never dies.'

It was perhaps the most eloquent epitaph that a non-revolutionary could possibly utter.

Turville, 2004

FURTHER READING

(For a fuller bibliography, see *The Fall of Paris*, below)

Allem, Maurice: *La Vie quotidienne sous le Second Empire* (Paris, 1948).

Bourgin, Georges: *La Guerre de 1870–1 et la Commune* (Paris, 1939).

Bruhat, Dautry, and Tersen: *La Commune de 1871* (Prague, 1960).

Costa, Gaston da: *La Commune vecue* (Paris, 1903–5).

Dansette, Adrien: *Origines de la Commune de 1871* (Paris, 1894).

Duveau, Georges: *La Vie ouvrière en France sous le Second Empire* (Paris, 1946).

Elton, Lord: *The Revolutionary Idea in France, 1789–1871* (London, 1923).

Goncourt, Edmond and Jules de: *Journal*, 1851–95 (Paris 1887–96).

Gorce, Pierre de la: *Histoire du Second Empire* (Paris, 1896).

Horne, Alistair: *The Fall of Paris, The Siege and the Commune, 1870–1* (London, 1965).

Howard, Michael: *The Franco-Prussian War* (London, 1961).

Jellinek, Gaston: *The Paris Commune of 1871* (London, 1937).

Marx, Karl: *The Civil War in France*, Introduction by F. Engels, Tr. E.B. Bax (London, 1937).

Mason, E.S.: *The Paris Commune* (London, 1930).

Rihs, C.: *Le Commune de Paris, sa structure et ses doctrines* (Geneva, 1955).

Thiers, L. Adolphe: *Notes et Souvenirs (1870–73)* (Paris, 1904).

Tombs, R.: *The War Against Paris, 1871* (Cambridge, 1981).

Vuillaume, Maxime: *Mes Cahiers rouges* (Paris, 1914).

Washburne, Elihu Benjamin: *Recollections of a Minister to France, 1869–1877* (London, 1877).

INDEX

watches Paris battle, 93
weapons
  French cannon production, 37–8
  French vs Prussian arms, 3
  Krupp's siege gun, 2
Wilhelm I, king of Prussia
  disturbed by cannon, 42
  Louis-Napoleon surrenders to, 1
  as potential emperor, 51
  proclaimed Kaiser, 55
  reviews troops in Paris, 69

war pessimism, 51
World War I, ix
Wörth, 4
Wroblewsk, Walery
  Commune commander, 103
  defends Paris, 133
  ideals of, 88–9
Württembergers, 43

zoos, 47
Zouaves, 1, 15, 17